WRITING FOR PSYCHOLOGY

Christopher Thaiss
George Mason University

James F. Sanford
George Mason University

Allyn and Bacon
Boston • London • Toronto • Sydney • Tokyo • Singapore

Vice President, Humanities: Joseph Opiela
Editorial Assistant: Mary Beth Varney
Senior Marketing Manager: Lisa Kimball
Editorial–Production Administrator: Donna Simons
Editorial–Production Service: Matrix Productions Inc.
Composition and Prepress Buyer: Linda Cox
Manufacturing Buyer: Suzanne Lareau
Cover Administrator: Jenny Hart
Electronic Composition: Cabot Computer Services

Library of Congress Cataloging-in-Publication Data

Thaiss, Christopher J.
    Writing for psychology / Christopher Thaiss, James F. Sanford.
      p. cm.
    Includes bibliographical references and index.
    ISBN 0-205-28001-3
    1. Psychology—Authorship.   I. Sanford, James F.   II. Title.
BF76.7.T43 2000
808'.06615—dc21   99-23803
                                           CIP

Printed in the United States of America

10 9 8 7 6 5 4 3 2 1   04 03 02 01 00 99

CONTENTS

PREFACE

Why this book? This book came about because psychologists write and psychology students write—and because writing in psychology is different from writing in other fields. It has many of its own rules, procedures, and traditions. This book identifies these, provides examples, and describes ways to make that writing enjoyable and successful.

Still, writing is writing. As you'll see as you read on, the lessons in this book also rely on some writing tools and practices that work for good writers in all fields, no matter how new or how proficient, whether for school, for work, or for personal enrichment. Chapters 2 and 3 guide you in the use of some of these versatile tools. We've chosen examples that adapt these tools to some typical, specific needs of the psychology student. We've tried to do so in a way that captures some of the excitement of psychology as a discipline, making it one of the most popular fields of study.

This isn't the first or only book on writing in psychology. No, earlier books exist and no doubt later ones will follow, because the need for good writing in psychology has been evident to people for a long time. But based on our reading of these earlier books, we saw a need for a concise volume that:

- Explained, with examples, how writers in psychology could use the best practices of good writers in all fields (Chapters 2 and 3).

- Explained in detail—again, with examples—how the successful psychology student created the three most basic forms of writing in the psychology curriculum:
  —the experimental laboratory report (Chapter 4)
  —the "term paper" and other evaluations of research (Chapter 5)
  —the exam essay (Chapter 6).
- Addressed the growing need of psychology students to become proficient oral presenters in classes and at conferences (Chapter 7).
- Offered a brief, easy-to-follow guide to APA (American Psychological Association) rules for citation of books, articles, and other sources, both in print and online (Chapter 8).

Honoring throughout the process model of writing, we not only give advice on correct APA formatting of information but also attempt to lead you through the decision-making stages on the way to the successful final form of the document. So you'll find, for example, that we annotate sample papers to show how the work demonstrates sound writing practices.

Who should use this book? *Writing for Psychology* addresses the writing needs of students at all levels of the undergraduate psychology curriculum, from introductory to advanced courses. It can also be used as a refresher and quick reference for graduate students.

ACKNOWLEDGMENTS

The greatest gift of writing is the opportunity it gives to work closely with others. This project has brought me once again into collaboration with my colleague Jim Sanford of the George Mason University Department of Psychology, with whom I have deliberated on cross-curricular writing issues since 1980. Jim's leadership and collegial spirit in writing across the curriculum have made his department exemplary in its attention to student growth in writing.

Brian Barker, poet and bibliographer, deserves thanks for the careful and creative research that helped produce our final chapter. Thanks also to the College of Arts and Sciences, Daniele Struppa, Dean, for supporting Brian's contribution to this project.

At Allyn and Bacon, thanks to Joe Opiela for his confident persistence, and to Mary Varney and Lisa Kimball for their efforts toward the success of this project. For their constructive reviews of the work-in-progress, Jim and I thank Scott Allison, University of Richmond; Dawn Reno, University of Central Florida; Victoria Sundin, Northern Illinois University; and Wayne Viney, Colorado State University.

My deepest thanks go to Irene, Ann Louise, Flannery, Christopher, Jimmy, and Jeff, who teach me as they grow, and to Ann, *amore mio*.

—Christopher Thaiss

The ideas that I have embraced in this book first began taking shape when I was an undergraduate student working in Harry Bahrick's laboratory at Ohio Wesleyan University and later, as a graduate student, working under the guidance of the late Sam Brown at Kansas State University. They were reawakened and broadened during my participation in George Mason University's faculty workshop in writing across the curriculum in the summer of 1980. There, with the guidance of Don Gallehr and Chris Thaiss, the concept of writing as a process finally became real. Out of that workshop developed a reading-writing group that met for years afterward. Group members Rick Coffinberger, Bob Gilstrap, and Erica Jacobs continued to criticize and encourage my writing efforts. More recently, I have received far more assistance than I have given from George Mason faculty and students far too numerous to name. But I would like specifically to acknowledge the help of Angela Bruflat and Jennifer Wilkinson, two of the best undergraduate student writers with whom I have had the privilege of working, for allowing us to use examples of their writing in this book. And, of course, a special thanks to Eric and Michelle and to Lyn, who always knows when to give me space and when to take it away and who remains the best editor of all.

—James F. Sanford

1

WRITING FOR PSYCHOLOGY

Welcome to psychology! If you have declared psychology as a major, you have joined a cast of hundreds of thousands of other students worldwide. Psychology is one of the most popular academic majors, attracting people whose interests range from mathematical modeling of human behavior to helping people cope with their difficulties. If you have claimed another discipline as your focus of study, or if you have not yet decided on your major, you will still almost certainly complete one or more psychology courses during your program of study. Psychology courses are taken by students in almost every major in almost every institution of higher education.

In your psychology courses, you will study cognitive processes and human (and sometimes animal) behavior. You will be trying to understand, as psychologists have since the founding of the discipline in the latter part of the 1800s, why we act the way we do. Your first course will almost certainly acquaint you with a broad survey of the history, methods, and content material of psychology. If you enroll in additional psychology courses, these courses will focus on narrower content areas, and they will explore these areas in more detail. If you major in psychology, you will also undoubtedly take a course or two in the methods and statistical analyses used in the discipline.

You will also be writing at every step along the way. As a student in an introductory survey course, you will take notes on class presentations. You may also be required to write one or more short papers or a longer term paper. If you attend a college or university that has relatively few students enrolled in each section of introductory psychology, your exams may include essays, and you may submit reflection papers on course content and how it has affected you in the present or past.

As you get to more advanced courses, the frequency and length of your papers will probably increase, and more and more courses will include essay exams. The writing style and format, the types of references you will have to include, and the depth and focus of your papers will also change. You will be expected to use the format and style mandated by the American Psychological Association, and your references will be expected to include recent primary source articles in professional journals.

DISTINCTIVE CHALLENGES ABOUT WRITING FOR PSYCHOLOGY

As you begin to understand psychology and what psychologists do, you will note one more important fact. That is that psychology is an **empirical** discipline. This means that psychologists have developed their knowledge base through observation and measurement of behavior. In their research, psychologists observe and record the behavior of humans and animals in many situations and in many settings. These settings include controlled psychological laboratory environments and real-world, natural environments. Methods can include laboratory experiments, correlational studies, case studies, naturalistic observation, and surveys or questionnaires. Even psychologists who do not actively engage in research base their practices on the knowledge that other psychologists have gained by using this empirical approach.

An empirical approach also requires that observations be **disinterested;** that is, researchers are expected to be **unbiased** in their recording of data and not influenced by their own hopes or expectations. (The term *disinterested* should not be confused with *uninterested,* since uninterested psychologists would certainly not engage in very much—or very creative— research!)

The birth of psychology is traced to the late 1800s, when Wilhelm Wundt established the first laboratory to study phenomena of the mind. Since that time, more than a hundred years ago, hundreds of thousands of psychologists have completed millions of empirical studies in attempts to discover what makes people tick. They have made careful observations and kept detailed records of behavior.

Prior to Wundt's work, philosophers reasoned about the contents and qualities of the mind but made few empirical observations of behaviors. These philosophers were students of the mind, but they were not actively seeking to **observe** and **measure** the behaviors on which psychologists base their conclusions about mental processes. It took Wundt and his followers to establish a new paradigm for understanding mental events. As students of psychology, you will hear of the empirical approach over and over, for that is how the discipline has come to understand behavior and mental processes.

What does this have to do with writing? In its most basic form, it means that a good deal of the writing that you do as a psychology student will be geared toward **describing, explaining** and **understanding** psychological concepts from the standpoint of **empirical investigation.** You will need to describe and critically evaluate research studies as well as describe the conclusions that these studies have led to. Textbooks in psychology routinely present descriptions and results of experiments and other types of studies as well as what these studies have told us. A survey of several introductory psychology textbooks showed that the number of references in them varied between 1,200 and 2,500, most of them reports of experiments, surveys, and other types of empirical research. "Just the facts, ma'am," is not enough. How the facts have become part of the lore of psychology is equally important.

Thus, in psychology, "creative" writing, at least as understood in English and the humanities, will occupy little of your time. Instead, your writing will be geared more toward explanations, summaries, critical reviews, and conclusions of empirical research. If the types of writing are put on a continuum, with **creative** (e.g., poetry, fictional prose) at one end and **technical** (e.g., scientific reports, laboratory summaries) at the other, most of the writing in psychology will fall in the technical half.

This is the primary reason why a book like *Writing for Psychology* has an important niche and why it should be a part of psychology students' libraries. Writing in psychology is not the same as writing in English or writing in business. It has its own focus as well as its own style and format. As you progress through your psychology courses, you will become more and more aware of how psychology works and why psychologists do what they do. Writing is an integral part of it.

WHAT THIS BOOK COVERS

Subsequent chapters in this book are arranged to proceed from general advice about writing that you can apply in all circumstances in psychology to specific chapters that detail the typical writing projects that face psychology students and working scholars. We do not suggest that you read the book from cover to cover, but you will find that later chapters refer you back to pertinent sections of earlier ones.

Chapter 2: Writing Techniques to Increase Learning, offers writing tools and exercises that will help you read more effectively and efficiently, will improve your observing and listening skills, and will help you develop your talents as a writer in varied situations. Systematic note taking, the reading response log, and the research spreadsheet are among the tools described.

Chapter 3: The Writing Process: Predrafting, Drafting, Revising, Editing will help you overcome writing blocks and anxiety, while also giving you strategies for more effectively meeting the often unpredictable expectations of professors who assign writing tasks. The chapter shows how proceeding systematically through a series of steps commonly used by professional writers in all fields can make the writing of all kinds of papers more enjoyable and successful.

Chapter 4: Writing Experimental Laboratory Reports explains the standard format of this central type of writing in psychology, but it goes beyond description to help writers negotiate the subtle differences among the parts of the report. While adhering to the standards of the American Psychological Association, the chapter illustrates through an annotated sample report by a student the ways in which an effective report takes shape.

Chapter 5: Writing Term Papers and Critical Evaluations of Research Papers builds on the tools of Chapters 2 and 3 to show how students and practicing scholars should analyze existing research documents in order to write effective critiques of that research. Through sample critiques, the chapter shows how writers define objectives for their evaluations and then communicate convincingly with readers.

Chapter 6: Taking Exams shows how students can adapt writing process techniques to timed writing situations both to (1) diminish the anxiety of test taking, and (2) organize essays to meet the expectations of professors. Sample student essays are examined.

Chapter 7: Oral Presentations adapts writing-to-learn and writing process techniques to helping you prepare to give talks that engage listeners while informing them. Telling-a-story and question-and-answer formats are illustrated. A section on tips for effective speaking offers a concise checklist for all situations.

Chapter 8: Brief APA Citation Guide is a concise adaptation of the documentation principles of the *Publication Manual of the American Psychological Association*, 4th edition. Original examples show how a range of sources should be cited in the text of a report and in the Reference section of a paper. Special instructions on how to include quotations in textual citations are also included.

2

WRITING TECHNIQUES TO INCREASE LEARNING

While much of this book explains formal types of writing in psychology, this chapter focuses on writing tricks and tools that professionals in this field and many others use informally to enhance their critical and creative thinking as well as their recall of information. These techniques should help you better understand and critically evaluate information from course lectures, discussions, books, and other sources.

A QUESTION OF ATTITUDE: WRITING FOR YOURSELF

Unlike the material in later chapters, this chapter discusses writing that will normally not be shared with others. When your goal is to improve thinking and learning, it's basic that you practice different writing techniques in order to discover what works best for you. This chapter will describe a range of tools and approaches, but you should think of these as starting points only and should evolve personally successful variations. Keep in mind that you will be the main—and often the only—reader of such writings, so feel free to try out diverse tools.

WRITING AND MEMORY: TAKING GOOD NOTES

When they are listening to lectures or discussions, people often regard note taking as a race. For fear of missing something, they try to scribble or type as fast as possible. Not only do they get fatigued quickly, but they miss much of what they try to hear.

Effective note taking should be carried out in at least two stages:

1. Quick **jottings** of key words or phrases during the course of a lecture or discussion, followed by
2. **Summarizing** as soon after the event as possible, while memory is fresh and the jottings can spark fuller recall. The goal of this summarizing is to organize the information in some meaningful way, perhaps chronologically or according to greatest significance.
3. A third stage, **revision,** may follow if you are reporting the lecture or meeting to another reader in a report. Chapter 3 details ways to make your revising effective.

Careful note taking according to this procedure forces you to concentrate on the *meaning* of the material rather than just the form or grammatical structure of its presentation. In 1972, Craik and Lockhart introduced the concept of *depth of processing* to psychology. They, and hundreds of others since then, found that people remember information better if they think of it in a meaningful context, especially if it is personally relevant to the reader.

Jotting Notes

The most successful learners often think of notes as a basis for further dialogue with a speaker or discussants. It may be useful for the note taker to assume the role of the **investigative journalist** or **science fair judge,** who not only is interested in accurate recording and useful interpretation but who also intends to follow up with questions about provocative, vague, or seemingly contradictory statements.

Accordingly, the jottings you make during an event should reflect *both* your interest in capturing the **main concepts** of an event and your observation of what seems **puzzling** or **inconsistent** or **unclear.** Frequent use of the question mark in notes lets you keep track of concerns that demand follow-up dialogue—or additional research on your part.

Tools

Technically speaking, while paper and pen/pencil remain the technology of choice for most note takers, laptop computers are becoming more frequent. As long as they can be used comfortably and without keyboard noise distracting those speaking and listening, they provide the advantage of facilitating revision of summaries into reports and other communications for other readers.

Using Visual Aids, Prewritten Outlines, Agendas

Jotting occasional key words during an event allows you to attend to the visual dimension of a lecture or discussion, which may be just as meaningful as the oral portion. Body language and facial expressions may give at least as significant an indication of emphasis or doubt as does what is said, and you might reflect this information in notes, too.

If a lecture or panel includes **material presented via overhead or computer projectors,** ask the speaker about access to those materials. Since the visuals usually indicate an outline of the presentation or the points the speaker wants to emphasize, having outside access can save you much note-taking time and will guarantee greater accuracy.

If an outline is given on a **preprinted agenda,** so much the better. This outline can guide note taking since it indicates some of the speaker's emphases and how the speaker has organized the information. An outline sheet can be used as a kind of **template** for notes, which you can use to elaborate on outline topics in the space available.

The Postevent Summary

Writing up your notes and other observations as soon after a presentation as possible allows you to expand on your jottings while the information is still fresh. The value of this exercise can't be overestimated, given the swift loss of many of these memories. Note taking during an event aids in retention, but it is no substitute for such a concentrated writing exercise as the **postevent summary.** Numerous studies of note taking show that it aids memory only if the notes are studied later.

The most straightforward method of writing up notes merely elaborates on the **chronological flow** of the presentation. A typical note:

Cog dev—Piaget—sensmot: 1st stage (0–2)

   early: sens & mot

      Obj perm—realize perm exist

Test: hide obj. child watch

might become:

In Piaget's theory of cognitive development, the *sensorimotor* stage is the first stage of development, lasting from birth to about 2 years old. Early in this stage, the child understands the world only through direct sensory contact and motor activities (hence the stage's name). Later, the child develops *object permanence* (knowledge that an object still exists even if not directly available to the senses). Now the child can think about things that are not present. Object permanence is tested by hiding an object (e.g., under a blanket) while the child is watching. If the child loses interest, object permanence hasn't developed; if the child looks for the object, this is evidence for object permanence.

This kind of summary is not necessarily an organized document, merely a fuller record of your observations. Nevertheless, it can serve as a substantial basis for later study or might be adapted into a draft of a research paper or report.

Alternatively, carefully reading over your jottings and thus "reliving" the event can give you a sense of a **center** or **focus** for your summary. Trying to find such a center is what the experienced news or sports reporter does after witnessing an event. For example, the concept of *object permanence* is a focus in the sample summary just given, since object permanence is an important development that changes a child's understanding during the sensorimotor stage of cognitive development.

Be careful, however, to read your jottings over closely before coming to an estimate of the focus. It's not uncommon for summarizers to read hastily and base their summaries on mere impressions rather than on careful rereading.

WRITING TO IMPROVE READING: MARGINALIA AND OTHER ANNOTATIONS

Writing in and on and about printed texts is a tried-and-true method for **remembering** and **thinking critically** about anything you read. If you are reading and trying to understand a book or xeroxed copy you own (and thus can mark up), always be ready with a pen or pencil to jot a comment or a question in the margins: top, bottom, or sides. Using this method of annotation is far superior to the popular—because too easy—method of applying yellow highlighter to any passages you think might be significant. *Writing* a comment or question gets the brain involved in thoughtful reading to a degree that mere highlighting can't approach. Besides, writing lets you express a wide variety of ideas and concerns about the text at hand; highlighting merely highlights. Sometimes readers unsure about which portions of a text might be more significant than others have highlighted whole paragraphs, only to find out on rereading that the highlights have not aided retention and certainly provide no new information.

As with note taking on lectures and discussions, text annotation works best if you regard yourself as being in **dialogue** with the author of the book, article, or report. While in most cases you certainly can't easily make the comments and questions known to the author, writing those comments and questions forces you to **focus** and **articulate** your thoughts about an idea you've read. Engaging in dialogue leads to a greater depth of mental processing of the information, and deeper processing is almost always associated with better comprehension and memory. These annotations can therefore (1) serve as the basis of ideas that you can develop into a formal piece of writing, and (2) help yourself understand *why* you found the passage worth remembering.

Making Annotation Effective through Critical Questions

Skillful readers read with one or several purposes clearly in mind, because definite purpose helps you concentrate on the reading. For example, you will read a software manual more effectively if you try out the software immediately and need answers to specific questions about installing and using the product. The skillful reader of fiction may want to compare features of an author's style to that of his favorite novelist. The clinical psychologist will read a case study more carefully if she has an eye toward understanding a client with whom she is working. A student fulfilling a textbook reading assignment can read with strong purpose, hence effectively, by applying well-known techniques for understanding and critically evaluating the information.

If your specific purpose for the reading is not already clear, the most common way to give your reading purpose is to **ask specific questions** to guide your reading and annotation. Here are **three basic critical questions** you can apply to your annotating, plus an example of the application of each:

Question 1: How Would I Summarize This Reading for a Person Who Has Not Read It?

The goal of this question is understanding the **main concepts** in the work. As you read, for example, the following excerpt from a cognitive psychology textbook by Karl Haberlandt (1997), consider how you'd answer a fellow student's questions: "What are these paragraphs about? What are the main points?" Use the margins of the page or a separate sheet (or a computer file) to take notes toward building answers to these questions. Observe how annotations have been used in the following example:

> Just and Carpenter assumed that the eyes reflect the mind's current work; that is, a person looks at the part of the stimulus currently being processed in working memory. Just and Carpenter called this hypothesis the *eye-mind assumption*.

What we look at is what we're interested in.

↓

"eye-mind assumption."

The investigators used an <u>eye-tracking technique</u> to monitor the subject's eye movements. They projected a small beam of light onto the cornea of one eye while recording the reflection of the light with a television camera. Through careful calibration of the recording equipment, the fixations and the movements of the eye were correlated with specific coordinates in the stimulus display. Using this methodology, researchers have discovered that eye movements are not smooth and continuous. Rather, we fixate on specific segments of a stimulus for durations of 100 to 500 milliseconds. Rapid sweeps, called *saccades,* of less that 15 milliseconds result in new fixations.

J & C's method.

"Fixation" is not continuous; <u>focus</u> moves.

Just and Carpenter (1976) recorded the eye movement patterns of subjects as they compared the Metzler and Shepard objects. Eye fixation records indicated that subjects switched their focus rapidly from one stimulus to another. The researchers distinguished three discrete movement patterns of the eyes: the search phase, the comparison phase, and the confirmation phase.

Three phases of focusing: search, comparison, confirmation.

During the search phase, subjects scanned the two comparison objects unsystematically. During the comparison phase, they looked back and forth between corresponding parts of the figures. During the confirmation phase, eye fixations started at the center of each figure and went out toward the ends, or the arms. (pp. 230–231)

Is our standard definition of <u>focus</u> this confirmation phase, or is "focus" this whole 3-step process?

The annotations show the reader **paraphrasing** (i.e., **using the writer's own words**) and **summarizing** the important points in the piece. They also identify points that might require further clarification.

Question 2: In What Ways Does This Work Comment on Issues or Topics That Are Important to Me?

If the work you are reading *seems* distant from your major interests, this question will productively test your imagination. Using this question, you watch for statements that bear on topics in which you do have some interest or intellectual investment. Marginal annotations can track these connections. Writing can be especially valuable as a tool to forge connections where there don't appear to be any—and thus where you might have trouble feeling motivated to continue reading. For example, note this annotation of the same passage from Haberlandt's book:

If the eye-mind assumption is true, maybe it can be used as a basis for determining how important certain things are to people. If people look at what they are thinking about, I should be able to measure how long people look at different things and estimate how important they are to different individuals.

Question 3: How Can I Simplify the Language of This Piece for Someone Who Doesn't Have a Clue about the Technical Jargon?

Using this question as a guide will push you to get into and through the technical terminology to better understanding of the concepts and details. Academic reading often remains opaque because readers don't make a concerted effort to penetrate the language. Readers often give up on difficult technical material, usually resigning themselves to their own inadequacy or to criticizing the author's style. Marginal writing forces you to slow down the pace of reading and strive to understand terms before moving on. For example, see how this annotation of the same Haberlandt passage guides your further understanding of the text:

Just and Carpenter assumed that the eyes reflect the mind's current work; that is, a person looks at the part of the stimulus currently being processed in <u>working memory</u>. Just and Carpenter called this hypothesis the *eye-mind assumption*.

As opposed to latent memory? If information is being processed, isn't every part of the affected memory "working"?

The investigators used an eye-tracking technique to monitor the subject's eye movements. They projected a small beam of light onto the cornea of one eye while recording the reflection of the light with a television camera. Through careful calibration of the recording equipment, the fixations and the movements of the eye were correlated with <u>specific coordinates in the stimulus</u> display. Using this methodology, researchers have discovered that eye movements are not smooth and continuous. Rather, we <u>fixate</u> on specific segments of a <u>stimulus</u> for durations of 100 to 500 milliseconds. Rapid sweeps, called saccades, of less that 15 milliseconds result in new fixations.

<u>Where</u> is the stimulus display?

"Fixation" is of incredibly short duration and is hardly distinguishable from movement.

Just and Carpenter (1976) recorded the eye movement patterns of subjects as they compared the <u>Metzler</u> and <u>Shepard</u> objects. Eye fixation records indicated that subjects switched their focus rapidly from one stimulus to another. The researchers distinguished three discrete movement patterns of the eyes: the search phase, the comparison phase, and the confirmation phase.

look up.

During the search phase, subjects scanned the two comparison objects <u>unsystematically</u>. During the comparison phase, they looked back and forth between cor-

Were these <u>saccades</u>?

responding parts of the figures. During the <u>confirmation</u> phase, eye fixations started at the center of each figure and went out toward the ends, or the arms. (pp. 230– 231)

But this "confirmation" still means continuous movement (almost).

WRITING TO IMPROVE READING: KEEPING THE READING RESPONSE LOG

While marginal annotation allows you to keep up a running critical "dialogue" with an author, you may also want to keep a **reading response log.** This log provides room for extended (or brief) reflection and analysis, which force you to process information more deeply. Moreover, by its nature, this ongoing collection of **dated entries** allows you to observe changes in your perspective and growth in knowledge. Indeed, later entries that summarize and interpret this progress are a characteristic of well-kept logs.

The reading response log is ideal for **research.** In Chapter 5, we describe and illustrate a specific type of log—which uses a spreadsheet format—to record data from research articles within standard categories.

Tools

Though the term *log* usually sparks an image of a large, hardbound book, more and more writers keep logs on computer. While the traditional book has the advantage of portability (an advantage somewhat minimized by the laptop), the computer lets you easily (1) **expand** and **revise** a strong entry or series of entries into a formal article or report, and (2) **send** an entry to a fellow reader via electronic mail. (The spreadsheet adaptation described in Chapter 5 can be kept in this way.)

Tips

1. Always **date** entries, including the year. Even if the current entry adds to an earlier one, date the addition.
2. When referring to specific passages in a book or article, always take the time to **cite the work accurately.** Though log keepers usually want to avoid delays in getting their thoughts about a work on to the page or screen, making accurate citations eliminates the later frustration of being unable to locate important passages. (See Chapter 8 for rules on citation of sources.)

Techniques

Think of the log as being as flexible, experimental, or structured as you wish it to be. Because the log is a **personal document**—usually for the writer's eyes only—most log keepers appreciate the freedom it gives them to **explore** ideas and **experiment** with different styles and formats. On the other hand, the log also frees you, paradoxically, to impose on yourself the discipline of specific kinds of critical analysis.

Investigation

On the side of investigation, the log can be similar to the **commonplace book,** an age-old tool of scholars and writers for collecting and commenting on interesting text that one encounters in the course of study or casual reading. The **writer's notebook,** wherein professional writers try out imitations of style and collect impressions of events and people, is another productive option for the log keeper. Even the experimental scientist or academic researcher can profit from keeping such a notebook. Your writing style will become more fluent and your overall writing ability more varied through such practice. Writing to Experiment with Style and Format (later in this chapter), contains two examples of informal writing done for this purpose.

Critical Analysis: The Scientific Notebook

On the side of greater analytic routine is the **scientific notebook,** that precise tool of the practicing scientist. In this form of the log, the scholar/ writer observes and records phenomena according to strict methods of the discipline. Indeed, many scientific notebooks cross the line from the private to the public document because they can serve as legal documents in cases of patent or copyright dispute or in cases of alleged fraud or incompetence.

Applying the Three Basic Critical Questions to Your Log

While we don't suggest that reading response logs should be taken so seriously in most instances, the log can be a good place to impose a regular analytic regimen on yourself. For example, one or more of the three basic analytic questions listed in the previous section can serve as stimulus for writing about reading. Say you are doing research for a report on the effects of fairy tale literature on early child development. Among your readings has been Bruno Bettelheim's *The Uses of Enchantment,* a classic and controversial study of this topic from a psychoanalytic perspective. Here's a possible application of question 1 to a portion of this reading:

Question 1: How Would I Summarize This Reading for a Person Who Has Not Read It?

1/12/99   *Dated entry.*

Bettelheim, B. (1976). <u>The uses of enchantment: The</u>   *Full citation according*
<u>meaning and importance of fairy tales</u>. New York: *to APA style (see Ch. 8).*
Knopf.

In his interpretation of "Hansel and Gretel" (a version
by the Brothers Grimm), Bettelheim elaborates on two
main themes: (1) the relationship of the main symbols   *Summary identifies*
in the story to the young child's oral fixation on the   *main ideas in reading.*
mother, and (2) the movement of the main characters,
the children, from dependence and fear to independence
and confidence. He uses this interpretation to illustrate
his argument in the book that these classic tales, usually   *Since the summary is*
violent and sexually suggestive, are important for   *written "as if" for a*
healthy child development because they honestly ex-   *person who has not*
plore essential themes in the unconscious mind. Adults   *read the essay, the*
who fear presenting these versions of the stories to chil-   *writer ensures that the*
dren, he argues, are deluding children and delaying   *entry will clearly*
their development.   *communicate with*
him/herself upon
rereading the log.

Notice that this summary might be translated fairly easily from the log into a draft of the report on this topic.

Creating Your Own Critical Questions for the Log

Similarly, you might also **create critical questions** to use as a regular framework for writing about reading. For example, it is common in scholarly research to question the credibility of an author. Therefore, standard questions for the log might be:

"What are the author's qualifications on this topic?"
"What are his/her experience and credentials?"
"What sources does he/she cite to substantiate any claims made?"
"What other evidence is presented?"

Alternatively, a log keeper might want to make **comparison** between and among the various sources a standard regimen for the log entries. This type of comparison is valuable practice for most writing in psychology, because **laboratory reports** (Chapter 4) and **term papers** (Chapter 5) include **reviews of the research literature** that depend for their effectiveness on comparisons of one study with another. For example, you might begin each comparative entry as follows:

> "_____'s essay agrees and disagrees with _____'s position in the following ways."

Here is a sample log entry that applies this formula to a comparison of Bettelheim's study of fairy tales with an essay on the same general theme written by Robert Darnton:

1/15/99

Darnton, R. (1984). Peasants tell tales: The meaning of Mother Goose. In <u>The great cat massacre and other episodes in French cultural history</u> (pp. 9–22). New York: Basic Books.

Darnton's essay agrees and disagrees with Bettelheim's position in the following ways. Darnton gives credit to Bettelheim for "some awareness of folklore as an academic discipline" (p. 12) and he calls his view of the symbolism in "Little Red Riding Hood" more "generous" and "less mechanistic" (p. 12) than that of fellow Freudian Erich Fromm. However, he criticizes Bettelheim for putting too much emphasis on the happy ending in the story, because the presence of a happy ending seems to have been a later addition to the French peasant folk tale, which has the wolf eating both the grandmother and the little girl—with no hunter coming to the rescue. To the extent that Bettelheim's argument about the value of folk fairy tales depends on the happy ending, then his argument is undercut by his choice of the Grimm Brothers' later version.

Note that this entry adheres to the exercise by showing <u>both</u> agreement and disagreement.

((On the other hand, it seems to me that the French peasant version fits Bettelheim's theory just as well, maybe even better than the Grimm version. Since Bettelheim's claim is that children can handle the violence and implied sexuality of these tales, then how crucial is the happy ending?))

Beyond just summarizing the points of the comparison, the log entry allows the writer to speculate further significance.

As you accumulate sources and comparative entries, you build an overall, integral sense of how all the sources contribute to your understanding the research on the topic—and toward developing your own educated, thoughtful views.

As emphasized earlier, the questions you impose on the log should follow directly from your carefully thought-out purposes for the reading. In psychological research, the most common purpose for reading is to evaluate prior studies that bear on your own research interests; hence, your log entries should address questions you create about the hypotheses, methods, and findings of the earlier studies. (Again, see Chapter 5 for greater detail on this type of analysis.)

WRITING TO IMPROVE OBSERVATION

Though every discipline relies on the ability to read critically, disciplines also demand the ability to observe and interpret other sensory data. The sciences and social sciences obviously demand the researcher's keen attentiveness to sights, sounds, smells, and the like. But the arts and humanities no less require a rich ability to perceive sensually and articulate those perceptions, for this talent is at the center of artistic creation and judgment. Writing can be a tool both to sharpen and to diversify our ability to perceive and understand sensual stimuli.

This chapter has described thus far three principal techniques for using writing as a tool of critical thought: **note taking, annotation of texts,** and **keeping a reading response log.** The section on note taking mentions that notes should attend not only to *what* is said in lecture or discussion but also to **body language**—and, by extension, other observed phenomena such as facial expression and tone of voice.

Both note taking and log keeping can be easily adapted to your needs as an observer of other phenomena. In this section of the chapter, we will suggest a few writing exercises that can make these tools especially effective in these kinds of observation.

WRITING DIALOGUE: AN EXERCISE FOR LISTENING

In this exercise, the writer's task is to record as closely as possible *exactly* what is spoken in a conversation and *how* the words are said. It's possible to use a tape recorder and then transcribe the tape, but the important act in the exercise is to write as accurately as possible. In striving for exactness, you must pay attention to what you hear—rather than, as listeners usually do, trying to penetrate beyond or "inside" the words for what you either want or expect to hear. Such an exercise is valuable training for any number of disciplines, including clinical psychology as well as medicine, law, law enforcement, nursing, and social work—fields in which listening to clients, patients, or other people is a necessity.

Here is a short excerpt of a dialogue, recorded in a student's observation log. Note the writer's inclusion of body language:

1/18/99

Dialogue with Irene (age 4) on Grimms' "Little Red Cap"

C: So, what happened in the story?

I: The wolf went to the grandmother's house and he ate her. Then Little Red Cap came and she said, "Oh, what big eyes you have," and the wolf said, "the better to eat you"—no, "the better to see you with." (Laughs). You don't eat someone with your eyes! (She puts her hands in front of her eyes and opens and closes her fingers as if the hands are mouths.)

C: Then what happened?

I: (Laughs.) Then she said, "What big ears you have!" and the wolf said (laughs), "The better to eat you with!" (Laughs).

To promote accuracy, the writer resists "editing out" so-called "mistakes," which might later be seen as meaningful in analysis.

CLOSE DESCRIPTION OF OBJECTS: AN EXERCISE FOR VIEWING

As with listening, seeing is often hindered by the human tendency to "correct" what is actually before our eyes toward what we desire or expect to see. One of us, to illustrate this tendency, routinely asks students early in a course to draw a face. Almost without exception, the students look only at the page before them and draw their *idea* of what a face looks like. It is the rare student who in fact looks at another person's face and attempts to draw what he or she sees.

In another exercise, students are asked to contemplate two or more very similar objects—apples, for example. Then they must describe in as much detail as necessary one of the objects so that **another person could identify *that* object from all the others just on the basis of the description.** Not only does the exercise demand close regard of the objects, it also challenges the writer to discover a range of **descriptive devices**—color, shape, statistical measurement, metaphor—to accomplish the fine distinctions.

Here's a sample close description following this model. Note the descriptive devices the writer employs to make the comparison accurate and vivid:

1/20/99

Orange 1

Stem: triangular, three petals surrounding a round center; each side of triangle about ¼ inch.

Texture: Pores deeper than on Orange 2, giving the orange a rougher texture. Several indentations near the opposite end from the stem give the orange an uneven appearance.

Color: mostly a yellowish orange, though with a slightly greenish tint on one side. On this same side, there are several brownish striations (indented) in three groups.

Circumference: 7 ⅝ inches at ends.

Orange 2

Stem: round, ³⁄₁₆ inch in diameter.

Texture: Pores very shallow, giving the orange a smooth texture; shallow striations radiate from stem area, and there are a few pocklike "craters" on one side; overall appearance smooth.

Color: uniformly yellowish orange; even the striations and craters are of this hue.

Circumference: 7 ½ inches at ends.

For clarity and precision, this writer chooses a <u>separate</u> description of each object according to the same list of categories.

Descriptive techniques include metaphors (<u>pores</u>, <u>petals</u>), statistical measures (e.g., circumference), and sensory impressions (color, texture), among others. The exercise allows the writer to choose any appropriate technique or category of comparison.

DESCRIBING A PROCESS: AN EXERCISE IN NARRATIVE

Here, the writer attempts to describe a brief process so that a person **unfamiliar with the process** can perform it. Such exercises, of course, are at the center of the scientific endeavor, since a basic purpose of the reporting of experiments is to enable other researchers to perform the same experiment. But **process description** is equally central to **teaching** the methods of every discipline; moreover, business success and effective government depend on the ability to communicate clearly **instructions** for everything from filling out tax forms to taking pain remedies to working a video camera.

Frequently, practice in writing process descriptions teaches a writer:

1. **Respect for different readers:** How technical can the language be? How can the writer inform the novice without sounding condescending?
2. **Close attention to even the smallest step in a process:** Testing process descriptions by attempting to follow them in real life usually reveals that the writer has overlooked small steps that are performed unconsciously.
3. **Diverse ways to "bring alive" a narrative:** Writers learn to give vivid examples, create interesting characters, use graphics and metaphors.
4. **Respect for feedback and revision—the "process" of writing:** The test stage of a process description almost always teaches a writer that one must go back to writing in order for it to meet a reader's needs. (See Chapter 3 for details on learning and applying these stages of the writing process.)

Here is a sample process description taken through several versions. Observe how we have tried to limit the use of specialized technical language and how the versions differ in terms of conciseness and clarity. (You might try out your own versions of this common process description.)

Sample Process Description: "Opening a Bottle with a Childproof Cap"

The message on the top of the childproof aspirin bottle reads: "To open, line up arrows on cap and bottle. Push cap up with thumb." Anyone who's ever struggled with some of these childproof caps knows that "push cap up with thumb" leaves a lot unsaid. More precise might be:

> Line up arrows on cap and bottle. Insert thumbnail in narrow space between cap and bottle; push.

Attempt is made to keep language simple, explanation concise and accurate.

Better yet:

> Line up arrows on cap and bottle. Insert thumbnail in narrow space between cap and bottle. Push with enough force to pop up cap without spilling contents of bottle.

For those with not enough thumbnail to wedge off the cap—or those who don't want to risk a broken nail—how about this?

> Line up arrows on cap and bottle. Grasp bottle firmly (for really tough caps, you may have to use two hands). While exerting pressure on the opposite side of the cap with the forefinger, push the ball of the thumb hard and with upward pressure against the arrow on the cap.

Notice that the attempt to achieve greater accuracy may mean a loss of conciseness.

To this might be added:

> If you are taking this pain reliever for headache, you
> may notice that your headache has worsened by the
> time you get the cap off.

WRITING TO EXPERIMENT WITH
STYLE AND FORMAT

A great way to learn from writing and have fun while learning is to experiment: to play with language, point of view, the appearance of the document, and the many other variables that go into writing. Up to this point, this chapter has emphasized using a log as a way to practice certain critical questions in order to make reading and other observations more meaningful. Here we suggest that an equally important function of writing, whether in a log or in separate exercises, is to do things differently from writing to writing.

While later chapters will present some standard **formats** for documents in psychology, keep in mind that the potential for writing in any discipline extends far beyond the standard or customary. Indeed, writers can't bring ideas to some readers without trying out designs, "voices," metaphors, or other devices that might strike some as strange or even wholly new. For example, just a few years ago the idea of composing business documents with sound and complex visual effects would have seemed like science fiction. But now, thanks to the enterprise and imagination of a few, Internet-based business, with most sites featuring just such effects, is a booming industry.

Writers have always had at their disposal a wide variety of options in style—reports, essays, stories, poetry, song, and drama are a few of the better known ones. Now, however, with widespread access to sophisticated graphic and presentation software, the average writer has choices that traditionally have belonged only to a handful of skilled artists and craftspeople. For example, writers who, regardless of formal training in art, work in the medium of the World Wide Web cannot only manipulate the printer's palette of font, sizes, color, and arrangement, they can also adapt the most sophisticated graphic—even cinematic—effects by importing material from other sites on the Web. A writer who creates an electronic folder of stylistic experiments is, in truth, creating an electronic log that teaches in the doing and that can be used as a sourcebank for other projects.

Even without employing computer technology, writers in any discipline can productively and enjoyably experiment with style and design. An excellent way to get started is to imagine how your language, layout, information, tone of voice, and other factors would have to change if a **radical shift in audience and purpose** of the document should occur. For example, using the description of Piaget's theory of early sensorimotor development from pp. 7–8, we can craft new versions that are meant for different readers and purposes.

Here is that description again:

> In Piaget's theory of cognitive development, the *sensorimotor* stage is the first stage of development, lasting from birth to about 2 years old. Early in this stage, the child understands the world only through direct sensory contact and motor activities (hence, the name of the stage). Later, the child develops *object permanence* (knowledge that an object still exists even if not directly available to the senses). Now the child can think about things that are not present. Object permanence is tested by hiding an object (e.g., under a blanket) while the child is watching. If the child loses interest, object permanence hasn't developed; if the child looks for the object, this is evidence for object permanence.

In experimenting with changes in style and format, consider some of the following categories:

- **Level of technical language:** What words need to be defined? For which terms should substitutions be made? Should some ideas be eliminated altogether or spoken about only in metaphor?
- **Tone:** play with mood: threatening, carefree, cryptic, earnest, fanciful, professional/technical, reassuring, etc.
- **Syntax:** short, simple sentences? long, complex ones? questions?
- **Person and voice:** personal and active ("I'd do X and so should you")? impersonal and passive ("research was conducted which might suggest . . .")? Consider how person and voice can affect the reader's respect for your ideas and interest in what you have to say.
- **Use of story and character:** "Imagine walking into a big room that smelled like . . ."; "Von Delbach stumbled on this technique when she was working on. . . ." Story and character usually increase a reader's attentiveness.
- **Conventional paragraphing vs. much indenting, use of bullets, boldface type, shifts in font and size**

Here are two versions of the Piaget summary that differ in purpose and audience:

Sample 1

These Piaget notes were rewritten to respond to a mother who is worried that her child might be retarded in cognitive development because of late onset of object permanence. As you read this version, think about its tone and how you might have to change it depending on, say, the degree of anxiety expressed by the parent:

> Piaget proposed that children go through sequential stages in cognitive development. Thus, the sensorimotor stage has to precede all other stages, and development of object permanence is a highlight of this stage. However, Piaget proposed an age *range* within which this development normally occurs, rather than a specific age. Children show many individual differences in how rapidly they move through Piaget's stages.

Sample 2

These Piaget notes were rewritten as a possible narration for a video for introductory psychology students. The video shows two children, one who has developed object permanence and one who hasn't:

> As you can see, Suzanne seems interested in the rubber ball. She is following it with her eyes. Now look what happens when, in plain view of Suzanne, the ball is hidden under the blanket in front of her. Notice that she looks away, apparently having lost interest. She has not yet developed the concept that the ball has an existence outside of her sensory and motor actions. Now let's watch Michelle. Like Suzanne, Michelle is showing interest in the ball. But now, when the ball is covered up by the blanket, Michelle actively seeks to find it. Michelle has clearly developed the sense that the ball exists even though she can't see it.

GOING PUBLIC: FROM WRITING FOR YOURSELF TO WRITING FOR OTHERS

The next chapter will describe techniques for transforming the writings you do for yourself into documents you intend for others. "Going public" with writing has often stopped would-be writers, who fear the scorn of readers. Keep in mind, however, that if you regularly practice the tools and techniques described to this point, confidence will increase as your skills grow and diversify. With practice, tools such as the log and a ready bank of questions for critical reading, seeing, and listening, there is no reason why you should ever be stymied by a blank page or screen.

3

THE WRITING PROCESS: PREDRAFTING, DRAFTING, REVISING, EDITING

When writing specialists talk about the **writing process,** they mean the steps and the attitudes through which a writer proceeds toward completing a writing task, whether it be a memo to a co-worker, a research report to a professor, or a letter to a loved one. Understanding how writers accomplish such tasks helps writing researchers improve the teaching of writing and the development of teaching materials.

GENERAL PRINCIPLES, BUT NO SINGLE FORMULA

In its details, the writing process varies for every person. Even the same writer will find that the process varies somewhat from task to task. To the composition scholar, the writing process also means a general progression of stages that is exemplified across the work of experienced writers, regardless of field. Though scholars have given different names to these stages of the writing process, they are most commonly referred to as **"prewriting"** (in quotes because we will be substituting what we feel is a more appropriate term), **drafting, revision,** and **editing.** Each stage will be described in this chapter. Chapters 4, "Writing Experimental Laboratory Reports"; Chapter 5, "Writing Term Papers and Critical Evaluations of Research Papers"; Chapter 6, "Taking Exams"; and Chapter 7, "Oral Presentations," follow the principles of **drafting** and **revision** described here.

"PREWRITING" AND DATA COLLECTION

Like anything else worth doing well, writing requires **planning** and invest-ment of a good bit of time *before* you sit down to make what will become the finished work. In the case of writing, this means that you should plan to do some, often considerable, writing before you actually **draft** the paper, re-port, or proposal. Chapter 2 describes such writing tools as the **reading re-sponse log,** which can be very valuable in this planning phase. Depending on how it is structured by the writer, the log can help you:

1. Plan the **content** and **organization** of any written work.
2. Sort through and **evaluate** readings and other data you plan to use.

As described in Chapter 2, the log can also be a place where you **experi-ment with style and format** for the project being launched.

The work you do before drafting is often referred to—somewhat mis-leadingly—as "prewriting." A more appropriate term would be **predraft-ing,** since, as we've seen, much writing is often involved in the planning stage of any project. Indeed, if you use this planning—predrafting—stage for log keeping, as described in Chapter 2, some of what you write experi-mentally in the log may indeed find its way into the actual draft.

Keys to successful predrafting are **patience** and an **open mind.** The more complex a writing task, especially the less knowledgeable you are about the subject and format of the project, the higher percentage of the to-tal project time you will need for predraft work. Don't be surprised to find that 80 percent or more of total time spent on a project will be devoted to the predrafting stage of, say, a piece of original research. Writing during this stage, perhaps kept in a log (as noted earlier), might include:

- **Notes** on lectures, interviews, conferences, or experimental procedures.
- **Annotations** in books and on articles.
- **Summaries** of notes and annotations.
- **Creative experiments** in style and format (see Chapter 2 for more detail on these techniques).
- **Analyses and interpretations** of research material or field observations (see the samples of log entries presented in Chapter 2 as responses to critical questions).
- **Mind maps (clusters)** of your ideas and observations about research material (see a description of this method of brainstorming and orga-nizing in Chapter 7).

Patience is vital in allowing this rich process of reading, talk, and analysis to shape the ideas that will be central to the draft.

An open mind is similarly essential. As Chapter 2 suggests, the purposes of the predrafting stage are **learning** and **critical thinking.** Writers who, because of haste or impatience, move too quickly to the drafting stage jump to opinions about data and then feel constrained *by the draft* from collecting more evidence and from doing fresh thinking. **Budgeting** sufficient predraft **time** and **using critical thinking tools** such as the log almost always ensure a better finished product, but writers need to be patient and willing to learn in order to be comfortable with these aids to writing.

Doing a Dummy Draft

One writing technique that can be part of the predrafting stage is what we call a **dummy draft:** not really a draft that incorporates all of your note taking and summarizing, but an attempt during your predrafting to **set down in an organized way what you have learned about the subject so far.** This dummy draft can be part of the log. Its purposes are:

1. To **bring together** the many details you have accumulated during predraft research in order to let you see what you've accomplished to this point.
2. To show you the **gaps, flaws, and inconsistencies** in the research, and thus indicate what still needs to be done.

Like the dummies constructed by engineers in the design process, this draft allows you to *test out* ideas and wording. The dummy draft is informal, its only reader the writer (and perhaps a close colleague who has agreed to give feedback on the preliminary work). This piece can help satisfy the writer's anxiety about the sufficiency and significance of the research to this point. It can also be **concise,** just long enough to achieve the two purposes noted.

To show something of the flavor of such a work, here is an excerpt of a dummy draft of an article by one of the co-authors about writing multiple drafts of laboratory reports in psychology classes:

Sample Dummy Draft

A large number of writing experts, both in psychology and English composition studies [put specific references here], have shown that multiple drafting of single papers is a valuable way to improve writing. It has been demonstrated that it may be more valuable than writing single drafts of multiple papers. [reference] Donald Murray (1995) has discussed revision as consisting of two separate processes. One is an *internal* process that includes the development of an understanding of the purpose and focus of the piece. It also includes a continuing modification, schema-like, of the writer's knowledge of the content material of the writing [this seems awkward, rewrite?]. the second, *external* revision refers to the actual writing that the audience will read [check to see if these are Murray's terms]. External revision develops from internal revision, and Murray says that a substantial effort to revise internally will result in a superior final product.

Murray's (1995) concept of internal revision relates closely to the use of multiple drafts. Feedback on a student's draft can facilitate the internal revision process. When a student revises a lab report based in part on feedback from an instructor, she can use the comments to develop new insights and understanding of the work. The writing process [processes?] includes learning and developing a fuller understanding of the writing topic. Feedback from an "expert" can only further enhance this process [these processes?].

Predrafting and Specific Writing Tasks

The following chapters will briefly describe appropriate predraft writing for such specific writing tasks in psychology as experimental **laboratory reports, term papers, timed essay exams,** and **oral presentations.** In general, though, our advice is the same, regardless of the task: sufficient time spent on such "working papers" as the log and dummy draft will pay off in better and more easily written documents.

DRAFTING: A CHANGE IN ATTITUDE

Moving from the predraft to the drafting stage involves a change in attitude and a large change in audience. The most useful attitude to take toward the varied writing in the predraft stage is one of **practical experimentation;** the main audience is you, the writer, and the primary purpose is **learning.** When you **draft** in earnest, the most useful attitude remains largely unchanged, since you must feel that whatever you are writing is only being **tested out,** and can be revised. However, the sense of audience has changed: now you are directly attempting to reach other people with definable characteristics as readers and definable needs for information. The basic **purpose** has changed, too, from your own need to make sense of the topic and other phenomena to **meeting the needs of those defined readers**—that is, the audience.

These changes mean that the drafting writer writes with a double consciousness: you write *both* with an open mind—that is, with an eye toward possible revision—and with a sense of **limits** imposed by the purposes and the possible readers. Thus, your draft has a very focused intent: "I'm writing this the way I want it to look to my intended reader." Yet you also feel the ease of knowing that this is not a final draft; hence, you can ask for

feedback—critical commentary—on this draft that can lead to productive revision.

Of course, "this draft" doesn't mean that the first writing you do for this new audience will be a draft that another person will read. Even after extensive predrafting, including the dummy draft, writers usually make many changes as the rough draft begins to take form.

How Rough Is the Rough Draft?

Unlike the dummy draft described under Predrafting, a so-called **rough draft**—another kind of working paper—should be intended to **stand as a final product,** unless feedback dictates that revisions are needed. In either academic or workplace situations, when teachers or supervisors ask to see a draft, they almost always mean a seriously written effort that incorporates the writer's best thinking and most thoughtfully analyzed evidence. A rough draft is like a rough diamond: not polished, but still a diamond.

That's why the so-called "rough draft" comes *after* the intensive work of predraft writing and research. Inexperienced writers often make the mistake of putting off the hard work until after the rough draft, which itself appears shoddy and which comes too late in the process to allow for the careful study and critical thinking that should have occurred before they ever began to draft the paper.

PLANNING THE DRAFT: THE THREE KEYS

During the predraft stage, writers should of course be guided in their study and planning by their thoughtful understanding of the **purposes** of the project. As illustrated in Chapter 2, the writer who has a clear sense of purpose will learn the most and think most productively about any subject.

Also useful in the predraft stage, but absolutely essential toward writing a solid draft, will be clear understanding of two other factors: **format** and **audience.** Along with purpose, these are the three keys of good draft writing.

Formatting the Draft

The **format** comprises both the **organizational structure** and the **appearance traits** of the draft. Sometimes—for example, when you are writing experimental laboratory reports—the format will be standard. For other types of writing, a great deal of flexibility may be allowed. For all writing, however, the format simply establishes parameters for the **types of information**

that can be presented and establishes limits within which the writer may still be creative.

Learning Highly Specific Format Requirements

If you are responding to an assignment from a particular reader—say, a professor or journal editor—**assume** that there are specific format requirements and **seek** to learn them. **Don't be misled** by the assigner's silence about format; he or she may be assuming that you already know all the rules. Then again, the assigner may have never given thought to what s/he expects—such readers often say things like "I'll know what I want when I see it."

There are two basic ways to **seek** the specific formatting:

1. Ask (see the checklist below).
2. Study and emulate earlier documents for the same purpose and the same reader. For example, grant agencies usually make available on request successful previous applications. Businesses keep files of their documents, which can be used by new employees as models of style and format; professors often do as well. And some faculty make available to students examples of model papers. *Caution:* Get the opinion of the person who assigned the task before relying on any earlier file as a model. Files may contain bad models as well as good. Show samples to the supervisor and let him/her choose the best to follow.

When you are asking about format, the following checklist may be helpful.

Typical Format Characteristics

Correct spelling, punctuation, and Standard Edited American English (SEAE) syntax: Assume these are required unless otherwise informed.

Order of information: Should the draft be organized in sections? If so, in what order?

Use of headings and subheads: Should sections of the draft have headings (titles)? What headings should be used?

Margins, spacing between lines, and indentations: Are there specific rules for these?

Boldface type, italics, underlining: What sorts of items should receive these kinds of emphasis?

Number of words or pages, minimum and maximum; type style (font) and size

Illustrations, photos, charts, and graphs: Are these required? Frowned on? Are there size and style restrictions?

"Special effects"—video/audio: Can video- or audiotapes accompany a written draft? How fancy should a web page be? If these effects are used as addenda, how should they be referred to in the written text?

Cover pages or cover letters: Should these be used? If so, what information should they contain, in what order, and with what appearance?

Footnotes, endnotes, and citations: Is a specific documentation style favored? How do the writers of model samples cite sources?

Appendices and other addenda: Are these allowed or encouraged? If so, are there page limits? How should data in the appendices be cited in the main text?

Quality of paper or other materials

Formatting on the Basis of Earlier Documents (Models)

If you can follow earlier models in formatting the new document, the checklist may also be helpful in analyzing the models. Do not hesitate to ask your intended reader questions about formatting, audience, or purpose that may arise when you read the model documents. For example, it's common for model documents to provoke questions about **formality** or **informality of tone,** about the **technical level of the language,** and about the **level of knowledge you should assume in the reader.**

Two General Rules of Formatting

In the absence of specific information from a reader or sample documents to use as guides, two all-purpose formatting rules of thumb can be used:

1. **Be simple and consistent:** Most readers respond well to clear layouts and consistent use of spacing, indentation, and other features; frequent shifts in font and type size tend to distract and confuse.
2. **Format so that readers can grasp your main ideas as quickly as possible:** Judicious use of headings, spacing, indentation, and emphasis (boldface, italics) guide the reader's eye as the writer wishes. Long paragraphs, tiny type, and little white space tend to confuse and (dare we say it?) bore.

Audience: Drafting for Your Reader

Unless you write only for yourself, you write for more than one audience: yourself and at least one other person. And even the audience of the self changes depending on mood, fatigue, and your latest experience. So drafting for your audience is no easy task, and it becomes more difficult the more readers who are involved. *Because your sense of audience changes as the project develops, don't be surprised if you continue to make substantial changes in your draft as you proceed. This ongoing revision is a normal part of good writing, one that experienced writers use to their advantage. Only the inexperienced resist this ongoing development of their thinking, tending to regard—even fear—it as a flaw in their writing rather than as a strength.*

Of course, the more practice you get writing for certain readers, the more you can assume about them and the easier the task becomes. But whenever the writer, no matter how experienced, tries to reach a new reader, some planning is called for and ongoing rethinking and revising of the work will improve it.

As with learning about format, learning about other traits of audiences might require **asking readers** and **using model documents.**

Talking with Readers (and Writers)

Don't hesitate to request further information about new assignments from teachers or supervisors. Some common concerns are those noted earlier:

- **Tone:** How businesslike? reserved? "official"? impersonal? friendly? solicitous? glib?
- **Level of technical language:** Which terms should be defined? Should any terms be avoided?
- **Assumed knowledge of topic or issue:** Should I assume that the reader has also read these studies? Does the reader already have a particular viewpoint on this issue?

By all means, be sure to ask the reader if s/he would be willing to give **feedback** on a draft of the project. Receiving such an invitation may be your best means of ensuring a high-quality final draft. (See "Feedback" in the Revision section of this chapter.)

Also don't hesitate to talk with **writers more experienced** in performing the kind of task you've been given. Even the simple question, "What should I look out for?" will usually provoke an informative response.

Learning from Previous Models

Besides using the formatting checklist on pp. 28–29, apply to previous examples the three sets of questions just listed about tone, level of technical language, and assumed knowledge.

An Audience Analysis Exercise for the Log

Before drafting, write an **audience analysis** as part of your log. Use this writing to think about characteristics of the various groups who might read your work. Make some preliminary decisions about tone, technical language, and assumed knowledge.

Here's a brief sample of an audience analysis exercise, as taken from a student's reading response log for the report on fairy tales and child development described in Chapter 2:

1/25/99

My audience will of course be Professor J., who has already told me that she has read Bettelheim, Fromm, and others on fairy tales, but who has also told me that she has read only the Grimm versions of the tales and has seen the Disney films of Snow White, Cinderella, and Sleeping Beauty. I think it's safe for me to assume readers knowledgeable about the Disney versions (I won't have to say that Sleepy, Dopey, and Bashful are dwarves, for example), but I'll have to be careful to show the differences between them and Grimm, and certainly between them and the peasant tales. I can probably just summarize B. and F. without going into a lot of detail on their theories, but I have to be careful to show in detail which parts of the Grimm and Perrault versions they are commenting on. I can leave in the Freudian jargon and won't have to explain it (I hope).

Knowing the Purpose(s) of Your Draft

The third key to good drafting is being sure of purpose. As with format and audience, **asking readers and experienced writers** and **learning from previous models** can provide insight about purpose. (See the previous sections on Format and Audience for details.)

Be aware that the purposes of any document are multiple. Even a two-line scribbled memo to a co-worker, "Let's talk at lunch about the research proposal," can have many intents, most of which may be indirect: (1) "Let's talk at lunch about the research proposal"; (2) "I'm including you and excluding _____ from our talk"; (3) "I'd like to have lunch with you"; (4) "I hope you'll have lunch with me"; (5) "This is handwritten and off the cuff; it's no big deal if you refuse"; and so on.

When you are talking to a reader or a more experienced writer, show awareness of these multiple purposes. Instead of asking, "What is the purpose of this document?" ask, "What is the most important purpose? If it does nothing else, what must it accomplish? What are some other purposes it should achieve?"

Again, as with audience, your sense of the purposes of a project will develop as you do more thinking and writing. The same advice about the

usefulness of ongoing revision applies to purpose as well as to audience. Always be ready to change your draft in response to your new insights about what you are trying to achieve in your work.

A Purposes Analysis Exercise for the Log

Before drafting the project, use this log piece to help you list and prioritize the purposes of your project. This **purposes analysis** may help you discover purposes of which you had not been aware; it may help you decide which information should come first; that is, in the position of greatest importance in most academic and business documents.

Here is a sample purposes analysis from the "fairy tales and child development" log:

1/27/99

> I'm trying to summarize studies that have been done on the influence of fairy tales on child development. B. and F. will probably be at the center of the study, because they are the best known, but I'll also be summarizing the theorists that they critiqued, and I'll be using Darnton, Tatar, Zipes, and others to show more recent critics and commentators. I want to make it clear that I'm not either agreeing or disagreeing with the Freudian analysis, but that I'm interested in showing how the study of folklore, which blends history with anthropology with psychology with literary analysis, makes any speculation about Freudian universals risky and subject to all kinds of cultural and situational differences. I guess that I'd like eventually to be able to write something for parents that encourages them not to be afraid of reading the old, violent fairy tales to their kids, but that doesn't minimize the impact of the stories, either.

EFFECTIVE REVISION

While any experienced writer would agree that "writing is rewriting," making that rewriting, or **revision,** effective calls for sound strategies, not just good intentions.

First, let's clarify what we mean by revision. Basically, writing specialists define **revision** as:

1. **Changes** that a writer makes to a draft *as* it is being written. As writers compose, they return to earlier portions of a draft and change the text in response to fresh insights; we've described this ongoing process in the previous sections on Audience and Purpose in the **drafting** stage, and we've shown in Chapter 2 a range of techniques and exercises for making this continual development of thinking productive. This definition of revision means, literally, your "re-seeing" a project and being

willing to make large changes in any and every aspect of the work. This definition of revision does not restrict it to a particular phase of the writing process. Rather, think of revision—this *re-vision*—as your willingness to change your work, perhaps totally, at any time during the writing process, if experimental evidence, further reading, feedback from a reader, or your own further thinking gives you good reason to believe that these changes need to be made in order to achieve greater accuracy or effectiveness.

2. A more **systematic process** by which a writer submits a draft to a reader or readers for **feedback,** and then makes changes based on reader commentary.

Revision is *not* to be confused with the copy editing, proofreading, or recopying that writers do before submitting a final draft to a professor, boss, client, or other reader. Such changes don't involve the thoughtful, often imaginative "re-seeing" that characterizes revision.

Why Do Writers Revise?

As part of the normal process of communication, more than one draft of a spoken or written statement is often needed for a message to be clearly understood. Inexperienced writers often wonder why writing over which they have exercised great care still fails to communicate. Experienced writers have learned that the need for revision is normal and not usually a sign of either the writer's or the reader's incompetence.

Moreover, experienced writers have also learned to *use* revision as a way to intensify and expand their own thinking. Trying out different phrasings, different organizational patterns, and different ideas changes your perspective on any task or topic. Using revision in this creative way often leads to a far better product.

Techniques for Effective Revision

1. Using Wait Time

Always try to budget some **wait time** into the writing process. The more time away from a draft you are working on or one that you have completed, the better able you will be to **see the work as another reader might see it.** In the midst of composition, your mind is likely so full of the ideas that you want to convey that it is difficult for you to detect gaps in reasoning or unclear phrasing.

Even overnight may be enough time for you to clear your mind sufficiently to allow for what is called **distancing** from a draft: that ability to see as others might see the writing. Wait time is especially effective in letting you pick up **vague wording** and unclear **transitions** from one idea to an-other. Of course, if you can set aside a draft for several days before reread-ing, all the better.

Many writing situations don't allow much luxury of time; rarely in psy-chology—or in any other field—is a document demanded the same day that it's assigned, however. Whenever you have any prior notice, or **lead time,** you would be well advised to draft sufficiently before the deadline to make use of wait time.

2. Looking through the Reader's Eyes

Using wait time to gain perspective on a draft is necessary for strong revi-sion, but it won't help much if the writer isn't able to see the draft from something close to the perspective that a primary reader of the text would have. The next technique we will describe is how to get good, direct **feed-back** from readers themselves. However, since all writers have to be critics of their own work, it's vital that you be able to "be"—at least imagine your-self to be—those readers.

Some ways to increase your empathy with readers include:

- **Studying documents of the same kind you are composing:** Good writ-ers in any genre are almost always avid, studious readers of the same type of work, whether novels or letters to the editor or research reports. As described under Formatting, finding and studying files of similar documents definitely helps in the writing process. If finding such files is difficult, ask the person who assigned you the writing task if samples are available.
- **Doing the audience analysis exercise:** (see Audience: Drafting for Your Reader): In the log or elsewhere, do one or more writings to help put you in the reader's frame of mind. Consider such questions as: "What does my reader wish to get out of this reading?" "What will my reader expect to see first?" "What would be likely to grab my reader's inter-est?" "What should I avoid in order to keep my reader from getting up-set or bored?"
- **Keeping handy the checklists of format, audience, and purpose crite-ria:** The more you work with lists of criteria, such as those given in the Drafting section, the more you will automatically apply these criteria. As long as you are still relatively new at working with a particular kind of assignment, it's important to keep at hand your carefully annotated assignment, log writings about audience expectations, and other notes.

3. Getting Good Feedback from Readers

Especially when they are facing new types of assignments or writing for new readers, experienced writers have learned how indispensable feedback from knowledgeable sources is to good rewriting. Carefully using wait time and keeping handy any written criteria always help produce better prose, but there is no substitute for specific advice from:

1. Readers for whom the document is intended.
2. Other writers experienced in that genre or with that type of reader.
3. Another writer whose opinions you trust to be careful and honest.

You should never presume that reader 1, also known as the **primary reader,** is inaccessible or unwilling to comment on a draft. For example, although college faculty in most courses do not mandate or even formally invite students to request feedback (though such invitations have become more common), almost all faculty we know are open to such requests from students and appreciate their initiative and seriousness in making the request. Similarly, while journal editors may not offer to comment on drafts per se, the process by which articles are considered for publication usually means feedback to the writer and requests for revision. Much material submitted to academic journals, for example, is neither accepted nor rejected outright; editors routinely send writers fairly substantial commentary written by themselves and by members of the editorial board, and these responses direct the writer's revision.

Another kind of **primary reader** is a member of a larger public who will be receiving a document and who will be expected to act in some way on its message. Everything from course syllabi to news releases to advertising is meant for such readers. Avoid characterizing such audiences in the mass, as "general readers" or the like. Instead, think of each hypothetical reader as an individual, with identifiable needs and characteristics. If at all possible, get feedback on a draft from one or more members of that readership. As with the first type of primary reader, give the reader specific questions that will focus commentary and show the reader that you want concrete suggestions—not bland praise.

Reader 2, the **writer with experience in that genre or with that audience,** can be invaluable in pointing out handy tricks and hidden pitfalls. In asking for feedback from such a source, be sure to specify exactly why you are seeking this person's advice. For example, "I read your latest chapter in the book you co-edited, and I know you've had a lot of experience writing articles like that. Will you read my draft and point out some things I should be sure to do and some things I should be sure to avoid?" Because of this writer's experience, you can rely on his/her being aware of most of the concerns you might have about format, audience, and purpose; this writer will be aware of other concerns that may not have crossed your mind. Be ready to listen, to answer questions this writer will pose to *you* about format and other issues, and take careful notes.

Reader 3, the **trusted adviser,** will be valuable to you mainly for this person's candor, the ability to write well him- or herself, and knowledge of how to communicate clearly with you. It usually takes much practice in asking for feedback, perhaps years, for a writer to identify a person with these qualities. Don't confuse a trusted writing adviser with a close relative or good friend. A relative or friend *might* turn out to be a good writing adviser, but it will take time for you to find that out. Never turn to anyone for advice just because that person is convenient to you or might feel obligated to give you some kind of response.

A note of caution: If you are writing an assignment for a psychology class (or any other class, for that matter), be sure to check with your instructor to determine how much feedback is allowed. Almost every course requires that some assigned writing projects be completed by individual students working alone. You should plan to seek as much information and feedback from others as permitted, but don't violate course requirements or honor codes in the process.

Some All-Purpose Rules for Getting Feedback.   Regardless of reader or situation, here are a few good ways to get high-quality feedback:

- **Always ask specific questions.** Before showing your work to someone, spend some minutes writing several questions that will help your respondent focus commentary. *Suggestions:* mark passages that you found especially difficult to write, then write out why you are concerned about the wording; ask the all-purpose questions "Where do I need to explain in more detail?" "Where should I cut?"
- **Make it clear to your respondent that you want constructive suggestions, not a pat on the back.** The least useful question to ask a respondent is, "What do you think?" Unless the person knows you well and knows that you really want honest, critical feedback, the respondent's tendency will be to make a generalized "feel-good" comment that won't help you at all. If you really do need some encouragement—and all writers do—ask the reader what, if anything, is strong in the draft and why. Then move on and ask your specific questions to spark definite suggestions for change.
- **Listen carefully, take notes, and exercise judgment.** Your attitude toward criticism should always be open, but it's also important to maintain respect for your own judgment. Listen respectfully to every reader's commentary, take notes on and beside your draft, but don't rush to change the draft until you have carefully weighed each comment. Even readers with similar backgrounds will rarely concur on all, even most, suggestions, so a writer should rely on wait time and on

his/her heightened awareness of format, audience, and purpose in order to decide how much critical commentary to follow.

- **If needed, get more than one opinion—but don't "shop around."** If you read the Acknowledgments in this book, you will notice that reviews of drafts of this guide have been sought from several people, all of them highly regarded in composition studies or in psychology. While it isn't usually practical for writers in most school or workplace situations to ask for a wide range of opinions, strive to avoid giving too much weight to one person's response—especially if that person is *other than* the professor who will be grading the school assignment or the supervisor who will be judging the proposal, and so forth. Reinforcing comments from several readers will give you confidence in the changes you plan to make.

    On the other hand, be careful to avoid mere "shopping around" for feedback. If the first person to whom you turn is an acknowledged authority on that type of writing, there may be no good reason to consult others. Moreover, consulting others may be interpreted as disrespect for the expert's advice and might jeopardize your future relations—and not only in terms of writing advice.

Some All-Purpose Questions to Ask Readers.   Remember that the questions you spend time writing about your draft, format, audiences, and purposes will be the best questions. Nevertheless, here are a few that work in most writing situations:

- **What comes across to you as my main point here? What do you feel I'm mainly trying to accomplish?**
- **What do you think I should write more about? What needs further explanation?**
- **What could be cut? Why?**
- **How would you characterize the person I seem to be writing for? Could you suggest any shift in my sense of the reader?**
- **What words or phrases seem to you unclear or misleading? Where are you confused?**
- **What questions do you have for me about the draft?**

Note that all of these questions must be answered with information, not a simple "yes"/"no," "okay"/"could be better" judgment. Your questions should show the reader that you expect to revise and need substantive help in identifying where and how to change.

EDITING THE REVISED DRAFT

Writers differ in their ways of attending to matters of formatting, grammar (syntax), punctuation, and spelling in the drafting and revision stages. Some writers need to keep everything neat and correct as they compose; misspellings and typos distract their thinking. Others write first, then tidy up the details just before they submit the document to the primary reader. Some do some of both.

Whatever the variations, most experienced writers give their revised drafts an **editing review** before submitting them to the reader. This pattern is exemplified in standard book publishing process: the revised typescript is carefully **copy edited** only after all changes have been made in the ideas (content) and organization of the work. Then, once the copy-edited text is set into *page proofs* (the actual typeset sheets in the font and size in which they will appear to the public), it is **proofread** at least once more to ensure that all errors have been caught (some are never caught, of course).

This final section of the chapter will deal with a few common errors in **grammar, punctuation,** and **spelling** within what linguists call *Standard Edited American English.* SEAE is the specialized dialect of written English in American schools, government, and business. As with all dialects, this one is continually changing, so don't be surprised to see occasional exceptions to these "rules" in some documents.

This chapter in no way substitutes for a comprehensive **handbook of English grammar and usage,** such as *The New Century Handbook* (Hult & Huckin, 1999). This section will alert you to a few of the *most* common errors that irk teachers, clients, supervisors, and other readers.

Three Common Errors in SEAE Grammar (Syntax) and Usage

Subject/Verb Disagreement

Rule: If the subject of a sentence is singular, the verb must be singular; if the subject is plural, the verb must be plural.

Wrong	The *Redwings is* the team that represents our town in the tournament.
Right	The *Redwings are* the team that represents our town in the tournament.
Wrong	The full *collection* of books, monographs, and letters *reside* in the university library.

Right   The full *collection* of books, monographs, and letters *resides* in the university library.

Vague Pronoun Reference

Rule: To avoid confusing the reader, do not use a pronoun to substitute a group of nouns not in a simple series. Readers will often not know to which noun(s) the pronoun makes reference.

Unclear   The Edict of 1245 superseded the Decree of 1218, *which* meant that residents of the kingdom had to register for taxation according to the value of land and livestock.

Clear   The Edict of 1245 superseded the Decree of 1218; the *edict* required that residents of the kingdom had to register for taxation according to the value of land and livestock.

Sentence Fragments

Rule: The subject of a sentence may not be a demonstrative pronoun (*which, that, who*), unless the sentence is phrased as a question.

Wrong   The candidate declared herself a native of Colorado, California, and Illinois. *Which* are the three states she lived in before going to college.

Right   The candidate declared herself a native of Colorado, California, and Illinois, the three states she lived in before going to college.

Two Common Errors in Punctuation

Comma Splice or Fault

Rule: A comma should not be used as connecting punctuation between two complete sentences.

Wrong   The company tried TQM during the early 1980s, it downsized drastically in the early 1990s and began outsourcing its training and accounting.

Right   The company tried TQM during the early 1980s; it downsized drastically in the early 1990s and began outsourcing its training and accounting.

Right	The company tried TQM during the early 1980s, *then* it downsized drastically in the early 1990s and began outsourcing its training and accounting.

Lack of the Second Comma in a Nonrestrictive Noun Phrase or Clause

Rule: When a comma is used at the beginning of a noun phrase or clause, a second comma must be used to close the phrase or clause (except when the phrase or clause ends the sentence).

Wrong	*Their Eyes Were Watching God,* a book by Zora Neale Hurston was widely criticized and ignored when first published but has become popular in recent years.
Right	*Their Eyes Were Watching God,* a book by Zora Neale Hurston, was widely criticized and ignored when first published but has become popular in recent years.

Two Common Spelling Errors

Misuse of the Spell Checker

While the spell-check function of most word processing programs will catch many spelling errors during the composition process, many writers either forget to use the spell checker or rely on it to do things it cannot. For example, a spell checker will not be able to pick up **wrong usage** of a **homophone** (a word that sounds like another but that means something different). The most common so-called "spelling" errors are actually uses of the wrong homophone (*it's* instead of *its, their* instead of *they're* or *there*). So you will need to proofread your documents carefully for uses of these words even if you use a spell checker for other purposes.

Hint: If you know that homophones give you problems, and if your word processing program allows you to do this, try **removing from your spell checker's dictionary** the homophones that plague your writing. In this way, every use of the problematic words will be marked by your program so that you may review the spellings.

Some commonly misused homophones:

it's/its	*their/they're/there*	*here/hear*
affect/effect	*discrete/discreet*	*flier/flyer*
where/wear		

and a near-homophone: *lose/loose*

The Problem with Spelling by Sound: The Schwa

The most common *kind* of English sound that is misspelled is the **vowel in an unaccented syllable.** Try saying the following three words: *pennant, independent, lesson.* Notice that the final syllable of each word has the *same* vowel sound, but that a different vowel is used in each case. Linguists call this vowel sound the **schwa,** represented in the phonetic alphabet by the symbol ə, a character not present in English spelling. Chances are that if you consider yourself a poor speller, a significant proportion of your spelling errors occur with schwas, because the correct vowel is not determined by sound.

Fortunately, spell checkers are great at picking up most schwa errors (except in homophones such as *effect/affect*), so use the spell checker. However, if you are not word-processing a document and if you don't trust your spelling, pay particular attention to those unaccented vowels and consult the dictionary.

A Final Note on Proofreading

Proofreading is no fun for most writers. To do it well, you must disregard *what* you have written about and pay *precise* attention to the tiniest details of appearance. Unfortunately, many readers place extremely high importance on correct syntax, punctuation, and spelling; even one error is sometimes enough to to ruin the strong impression created by your careful predraft efforts, drafting, and revision. (Did you notice the error in the preceding sentence?) Consequently, careful proofreading is an absolute must for any document you want to win a reader's interest and good will, so time in the writing process must be reserved for this final, equally important stage.

Proofreading for Spelling Errors

If you are not writing on a word processor with a spell-check program, the best way to check for spelling errors is the tedious but effective technique of **reading your text backward, one word at a time.** In this way, you can concentrate on each word because you will not get caught up in the flow of ideas. But remember to stay alert for misused **homophones** (see previous page); remember, too, that this technique only works for spelling—it can't help you catch any other kind of error. (See the Editing section earlier for other tips on checking for spelling errors.)

Proofreading for Errors in Punctuation and Syntax

See the Editing section and keep it handy when you proof your documents. The common errors noted there are often missed by even the most sophisticated grammar-checking programs on computer word processors.

Nevertheless, we strongly recommend the most recent versions of such grammar-checking programs because they are adept at catching such common errors as repetition of the same word (*to to*), too much spacing between words, wrong punctuation, and the frequent failure of writers to remember that a change in one part of a sentence means that they must change other parts of the sentence for syntax to be consistent. For example, it's common for a writer to change a plural noun to a singular noun and forget to change the verb correspondingly.

But **use grammar checkers cautiously.** Not only do they miss much more than they pick up, they also alert you to many possible errors that are in fact correct constructions. So tend to trust your own judgment more than that of the computer. The best editors are human; in any workplace where correct writing is important, good editors are worth their weight in gold.

4

WRITING EXPERIMENTAL LABORATORY REPORTS

LAB REPORTING: A CENTRAL SKILL

Almost every four-year college and university requires its psychology majors to complete an experimental laboratory course. Sometimes this course covers a broad spectrum of content material, including sensation, perception, learning, memory, and other cognitive processes. Sometimes the content is more focused toward a specific area of experimental psychology, such as learning or memory and cognition. But regardless of the curriculum, as a psychology major you can count on writing a number of experimental laboratory reports.

Writing lab reports is a vital skill for all psychology majors, especially those who plan to further their education in graduate school or seek employment in a research setting. Writing can be used as a tool throughout the experimental process, from

- careful **note taking** during the literature review
- to careful exposition of **directions to participants**
- to well-crafted **drafting** of the report.

Writing in experimental psychology laboratory courses often involves **multiple drafting** (see Chapter 3). Since a standard format is used for experimental reports, **rewriting** after receiving feedback from the lab instructor can be especially helpful in improving later drafts and later reports.

You should also be aware that the experimental psychology course often comes with a well-deserved reputation as the single most work-intensive course in the psychology curriculum. It usually involves laboratory work—including designing and running experiments, completing statistical analyses, and writing lab papers—in addition to the reading, papers, and exams found in a regular content course.

APA STYLE AND FORMAT GUIDELINES

You will almost certainly write your laboratory reports in a style and format mandated by the American Psychological Association (APA) in the *Publication Manual of the American Psychological Association,* usually abbreviated as the APA manual. The first APA manual appeared in 1952 and established a tradition of style and format recognized for journal publications in psychology and a number of other disciplines. Later editions were published in 1974, 1983, and 1994. Portions are now available on the Internet. While the manual doesn't address all issues of writing style, it is relatively prescriptive in specifying the format of a published paper. All students who plan to write research articles should have access to the latest edition of the manual. Furthermore, we recommend that students purchase their own copies of the manual if they plan to continue their education in graduate school or involve themselves in psychological research beyond the experimental psychology course. It is available in most college bookstores or through the American Psychological Association. Copies may be ordered from APA Order Department, P.O. Box 2710, Hyattsville, MD 20784.

When students are first introduced to the APA style and format used in laboratory reports, they often feel a bit intimidated. Everything from how to report statistical analyses to how to construct a title page is discussed. However, nobody should expect to learn all the nuances of APA report writing. Nearly all professionals who publish research articles in journals that use APA style and format have their own copy of the manual because they know that they will have to use it from time to time. It is a reference book, just like a dictionary or thesaurus, and, like other references, should be used when questions arise.

Even if you do not plan on graduate school or a career involving publishing, it is still important to understand the basics of APA style and format. General familiarity with APA style and format can save experimental report writers a lot of time. Just like a dictionary or a thesaurus, the APA Publication Manual should have to be referenced only occasionally.

STANDARD FORMAT OF THE
LABORATORY REPORT

All experimental reports include the following elements:

- **Title page**
- **Abstract**
- **Introduction**
- **Section describing the research methods used**
- **Results section**
- **Discussion section**
- **Section containing the references used in the text of the article**

Each section has a specific function and, frequently, a recommended order in which different types of information are presented. This structure can serve as a **mental schema** for both writing and understanding experimental reports. This means that writers can use the format prescribed by APA to focus their thoughts and organize the points they are attempting to make. Since the structure of a lab report is fixed, writers who are familiar with this structure have a built-in outline for their reports. Thus, experienced report writers can emphasize content rather than organization in their writing.

The remainder of this chapter will deal with writing each section of an experimental report. It will not, however, go into detail about specific format issues, which are addressed in detail in the APA manual. Many textbooks on research design and procedure also include a chapter on APA report writing.

SECTION 1: TITLE PAGE

The title page includes the **title** of the manuscript, the **author's name,** the **institutional affiliation** of the author, a **manuscript page header,** and a **running head.**

The **title** should identify as precisely as possible the topic of investigation. It often specifies the actual variable or variables being studied. The APA manual recommends that titles be about 10 to 12 words in length. The line (or lines) that include the title, just like lines containing the author and institutional affiliation, should be centered.

The **author's name** is usually given as first name, middle initial, and last name. The **institutional affiliation** identifies where the study was completed.

The **manuscript page header** is a very short abbreviation of the title that is used to keep track of article pages during the review process. This **page header** appears at the top of every page of the submitted manuscript, but it does not appear in the printed version of an article. You should check with your instructor to see if you should include it when you are preparing a report for class.

The **running head** is an abbreviated form of the title. It is included on the title page, on the line below the page header and page number, because most psychology journals include it on pages of a published article. If you open a psychology journal and look at the two facing pages, you should find the author's name on the top of one and the running head on the top of the other. Running heads are limited to a maximum of 50 characters.

Please also notice that every page of a manuscript includes a page number, starting with the title page.

Sample Title Page

Here is a sample title page from a paper written by Angela Bruflat, a recent student in a laboratory course in human memory and cognition at George Mason University. Successive sections of Angela's paper will be presented after the content and format of each section of a laboratory report are discussed. By the end of this chapter, you will have seen Angela's complete experimental laboratory report.

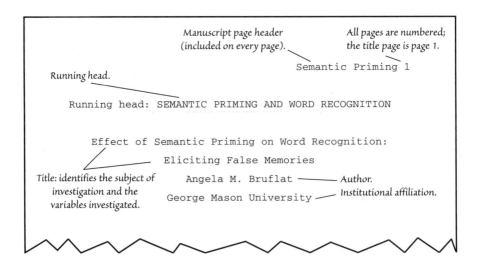

SECTION 2: ABSTRACT

We will describe this section later (pp. 68–70), after the other sections of the report have been explored, because it is the final section of text to be *written* (drafted), even though it is the first *presented* in the finished manuscript.

SECTION 3: INTRODUCTION

The **Introduction** to the report identifies why the study was done, within the context of a historical overview. It usually includes, in order, the following elements:

- **Introduction to the topic**
- **Concise discussion** of previous literature that has addressed the problem being studied
- **Statement of the hypotheses** and how they were derived from previous research
- **Broad overview of the method** used in the study

Good introductions usually use an **inverted triangle** approach. This means that the beginning of the introduction is broad, introducing issues being studied from a historical and conceptual point of view. The focus is then narrowed as the investigator addresses the relationship between previous studies and present research. As the end of the introduction approaches, the focus narrows further still to the specific hypotheses being tested and the general methods used to test them.

Introduction to Topic

The first paragraph or so of an Introduction begins to develop background information. Here, the reader is presented with a brief description of the general topic of interest and how it has been addressed in previous research. It is the most general part of the Introduction and alerts the reader to the main issues that are going to be addressed later in the section and in the research itself. Brief summaries of relevant previous work may be described, but only in a general way. A more detailed examination of previous research is deferred until later paragraphs of the Introduction. (As we describe the parts of the Introduction, you may wish to refer to the sample report, "Effect of Semantic Priming on Word Recognition: Eliciting False Memories," which begins on p. 51.)

Concise Literature Review

After the general topic has been delineated, the next section of an Introduction presents a concise and focused review of what other investigators have found. The research that is summarized here should be directly related to your experiment. An experimental report is not the place to present an exhaustive summary of previous research. More general reviews are left for review articles and books. **It is a good idea to check with your lab instructor to determine how detailed your literature review should be.** However, research reports for APA journals must be written with an eye toward conciseness. Readers can refer to articles cited in the manuscript and complete a more general literature search for further information on the topic of the report.

Avoid Mere Chronology in the Literature Review

An important consideration in describing relevant literature is how to structure the review. All too often, students will present a **chronological** summary, starting with the earliest study cited in the paper and ending with the most recent. However, this type of organization usually fails to provide a clear focus on the issue under discussion. It also leads to text that is difficult to understand because studies that are discussed in chronological order often address different research issues.

A much better structure for the literature review is to organize by **topic.** This organization entails grouping related studies together and discussing their general conclusions. For example, if different groups of studies have led to different conclusions, organizing your literature review by this grouping allows the reader to compare and contrast the bases for the differences. It is easier for the reader to understand why the study is important and how it is related to your research.

Relationship of Study to Topic

The middle paragraphs of the Introduction are the place to develop the specific problem addressed in the current study. Here an investigator points out why additional research is needed and where his or her proposed study addresses this need. This is also the place to point out possible weaknesses in earlier studies. These perceived shortcomings often form the basis for later research. *But a note of caution:* Remember that psychology has developed its knowledge of behavior and cognitive processes by empirical observation. Therefore, researchers should be careful to justify their criticisms by specifying possible **methodological weaknesses, inconsistencies** between the predicted and obtained outcomes, **questions** about how variables were operationalized, and so on. Research reports should not include unsupported personal opinions and arguments.

Hypothesis Statement

Now it is time to state your hypotheses and to briefly introduce the procedures you used to test them. The basis for these hypotheses was developed in the earlier paragraphs of the Introduction, and the reasons for undertaking your study should make sense to the reader by the time they are stated. Remember that your research hypotheses state the bases for your study. It is important to be explicit in stating them.

Your description of the procedure you used to test your hypotheses should be brief, only long enough to inform the readers in a general way of how you operationalized your research questions. By the end of the Introduction, the reader should have a good sense of **why you completed the study, what niche it fills** in the development of a knowledge base in psychology, and **what you predict the outcome to be.**

Using Writing-to-Learn Techniques in Predrafting the Report

Before you can draft the parts of the Introduction, you'll need to use techniques described in Chapter 2, including accurate note taking and summarizing of material you read.

Taking Notes on Research Literature

Writing an Introduction to an experimental report is more than summarizing work that you have already done. It also includes **note taking during a**

literature search. As we have described, part of the Introduction summarizes what other investigators have found and the ways they have found it. When you undertake your literature review, you must be very careful to maintain complete and accurate notes. These include accurate title, author, and journal citations as well as careful summary of the studies. During your search, you may observe that when different methods were used, different outcomes were obtained. But in order to make this connection between method and outcome, you must take care to state the methods that each researcher used. Thus, writing to learn occurs during the literature review process.

Summarizing to Achieve Focus

Writing an Introduction can also include **writing to come up with an idea for a research topic.** Frequently, when reading and taking notes on previous literature, you discover a new direction for your proposed research. By summarizing and putting in context the work of others, you generate new and creative ideas.

Sample Introduction

On the next pages is the annotated sample Introduction from Angela Bruflat's paper. Angela's paper describes an experiment she did that investigated the "false memory effect." This effect occurs when people incorrectly "remember" words that they did not study but that are closely related to other words that they are instructed to remember. For example, if a list of words included *tree, forest, leaf, grass,* and *vines,* a person might falsely remember that the word *woods* was included in the list.

In reading the Introduction section, you should be able to recognize that Angela has used the inverted triangle approach, starting with a broad introduction to the topic and narrowing to specific statements about the experimental hypotheses and the method she used to investigate the research issue. The remaining sections of Angela's paper will be presented after each of the respective sections is introduced. By the end of this chapter, you will have seen Angela's complete experimental laboratory report. Please note that in an actual submission, the title page and the abstract are always contained on pages 1 and 2, respectively. After that, the main body of the paper is presented in continuous fashion; there are no page breaks between sections. Only the Reference section and tables and figures stand by themselves on pages specifically dedicated to them.

Effect of Semantic Priming on Word Recognition:
Eliciting False Memories

Research on false memory dates back to
Bartlett (1932) and his distinction between
reproductive (rote and accurate) and
reconstructive (error-prone due to creating
missing details) memory. There has been a
recent resurgence in the interest in false
memories among psychologists and the general
public. The increased attention to the subject
of false memories stems largely from the
growing number of allegedly recovered memories
of past child abuse. The truth behind some of
these allegations has been questioned. Recent
research has supported the existence of false
memories which participants are confident are
true.

*The Introduction
section begins with a
general introduction
to false memory.*

Roediger and McDermott (1995) completed a
number of experiments investigating false
memories. In them, participants listened to
lists composed of words which all related
strongly to one word which was absent from the
list (referred to as the critical lure). For
example, the critical lure for the list
containing words such as "bed," "rest,"
"tired," "dream," and "slumber" is "sleep."
Roediger and McDermott administered both free
recall and recognition tests and found that the
critical lures were recalled at about the same
rate as the actual words that appeared in the
middle of the lists. Since the rate of falsely
recalling non-lure words was significantly
lower than the rate of recalling critical
lures, Roediger and McDermott concluded that
the recall results could not be due to mere
guessing. On the recognition test, critical
lures were recognized at a rate that was

*Concise literature
review begins with
the most important
studies of the
specific topic under
investigation.*

comparable to the list words but significantly larger than the rates for weakly related words and unrelated words that were not on the list. Roediger and McDermott also found that participants were very confident that critical lures were on the studied list. They offered several possible explanations for the high rates of false recall and recognition of the critical lures. One of their explanations involved a network model of long-term memory that proposes that long-term memory for words and concepts is made up of interconnected nodes that are organized by semantic similarity (Collins & Loftus, 1975). According to this model, there is a spreading activation among connections. This spreading activation can explain why the critical lure was falsely recognized. The numerous related words presented beforehand make the critical lure much more accessible.

In a second experiment, Roediger and McDermott (1995) instructed participants to label each word that they recognized with either an R (remember) or a K (know). The R signified that the participants could specifically recall the word being presented and specifically recall an aspect of its presentation, such as what they thought of when they heard the word. The K signified that the participant felt certain that the word was on the presented list but could not specifically remember studying the word. Another modification in Roediger and McDermott's second experiment was that some participants completed a recall test before a recognition test while a second group was only required to recognize the words. Roediger and McDermott found that

Semantic Priming 5

recognition rates for critical lures and list words were similar. In addition, the act of recall increased both recognition of old words and false recognition of critical lures as well as the percent of R judgments assigned to critical lures. Roediger and McDermott concluded that the increase in remember responses for critical lures that followed recall tests could be due to participants' memory of the experience of recalling the word rather than studying it.

Read (1996) employed the same basic design as Roediger and McDermott (1995) but manipulated encoding instructions. One-third of the participants were assigned to the serial learning condition, and they were instructed to focus on remembering the words in the exact order of presentation. The elaborative-learning participants were instructed to think about and rehearse the words in a manner that would enhance their responses to questions about word meanings. Maintenance-rehearsal participants were told to keep the last word presented in mind. In addition, half the participants in each encoding condition completed a free recall test while the other half completed a serial recall test (that is, they were instructed to recall the words in the same order as they were presented). Read found that the elaborative-rehearsal group recalled significantly more list words than the maintenance-rehearsal group and that the latter group recalled significantly more than the serial-learning group. In addition, the elaborative-rehearsal and maintenance-rehearsal groups had similar recall rates for the critical lures, both of them higher than that of the serial-learning

Other relevant research—arranged by topic.

group. There was no significant difference
across the type of test that the participants
had to complete.

Read (1996) concluded that associations to
a a particular words do not arise during
retrieval because the retrieval method had no
effect on frequency of false memories. In line
with the network model, Read postulated that
since the list consisted of words related to
the critical lure, this lure may have been
activated (via interconnections in the network)
early in the list. Subsequent associated words
in the list continued to elicit the critical
lure, which reinforced its probability of being
recalled.

McDermott (1996) investigated the effect of
delaying testing on false memories. One group
took an immediate recall test, another took a
delayed test (this group solved math problems
between list presentation and recall), and a
third completed no test (solved math problems
after list presentation). Two days later, all
three groups completed a free recall test.
McDermott found that the initial recall tests,
taken on the day the lists were studied, showed
no difference in the critical lure recall
rates. However, the rates for recall of list
words declined with short time delay. The tests
completed two days later resulted in higher
recall rates of both critical lures and list
words for groups that had completed an earlier
recall test. Regardless of the condition,
recall rate of critical lures was significantly
higher than recall rate of list items after a
two-day delay.

McDermott (1996) concluded that the testing
effect (the act of recall enhancing subsequent

*Discussion of an
additional study of
false memory.*

recall) exists for false recall. She suggested that the critical lures were retrieved from long-term memory just as old words were. However, she does not offer an explanation for why critical lures were recalled at higher rates than actual list words.

McDermott's (1996) results were corroborated by Payne, Elie, Blackwell, and Neuschatz (1996) who offered a "fuzzy trace" explanation of the false memory effect. "Fuzzy trace" suggests that a gist representation is established and that retrieval is based on a general schematic content rather than a verbatim representation of the words that were studied (Brainerd & Reyna, 1990). Payne et al. proposed that while words are read aloud, participants store verbatim representations as well as gist representations that encode the overall pattern of meaning of the list. Since every item on the list relates to the critical lure, the gist representation conveys information that list items share a common theme. From this perspective, it makes sense that the critical lures would be remembered better over time since the critical lure represents the central focus of the list. This explanation is in line with previous research that has shown the main points, or gist, of words and passages are likely to be remembered over time while accurate memory for specific details declines (Alba & Hasher, 1983; Bransford & Franks, 1971).

The present experiment was intended to replicate parts of Roediger and McDermott's (1995) series of experiments. The purpose was to determine if the recognition rates for critical lure words would be equivalent to or

Description of a possible explanation of the false memory effect. Note that this explanation is presented to account for all the research described above. It is not presented as part of each individual study, thus ensuring that the Introduction section is organized by topic.

The focus narrows: a description of the bases for the study reported in this paper.

greater than the recognition rates for list
words. In the experiment, participants listened
to six lists of twelve words each. After each
list was read, participants completed a recall
test, then a distractor task, and finally a
recognition test containing list words, related
new words, unrelated new words, and critical
lure words. Participants were instructed to
label each word that they recognized with
either an R or a K.

A brief introduction to the method used.

　　In accordance with the network model, we
expected the unrelated and weakly related new
words to have much lower recognition rates than
critical lures. This was expected because
spreading activation among semantically related
nodes should prime the critical lure (that is,
make it more accessible) but not prime the
other words because their nodes are located
farther apart in the network (Collins & Loftus,
1975). We also expected the recognition rates
for critical lures to be similar to that of
list words rather than greater because enough
time would not have elapsed for participants to
forget a significant number of the specific
words that were presented (McDermott, 1996;
Payne et al., 1996).

Statement of hypotheses.

SECTION 4: METHOD

The **Method** section provides the reader with a detailed account of what
you did. It includes sufficient detail to allow another researcher to essentially replicate (that is, rerun) your experiment. This detail is also necessary
to allow readers to evaluate the strengths and weaknesses of your methodology. (After all, you may have completed your experiment because you
pointed out flaws in the methods of other studies!)

The Method section is usually divided into three subsections: **participants, apparatus** or **materials,** and **procedure.**

Subsection I: Participants

The **Participants** subsection is usually quite short and describes who participated in your experiment. Please note that the term *subjects* is no longer used when writing in APA style if human beings participated in the research; *subjects* is now a term reserved for animals. The description of the participants should be sufficiently specific to identify the population to which the results can be generalized. For example, a Participants subsection that includes the statement "32 people with schizophrenic disorder" indicates that the population of interest is people with schizophrenic disorder. Often, some major demographic characteristics are included (e.g., the range of ages or the mean age; the number of women and men who participate), but a great deal of detail is not necessary unless a demographic characteristic is one of the variables being studied or might be important in identifying the generalizability of the results. Thus, if you are comparing performance of students whose native language is English to those whose native language is Spanish, the distribution of English-to-Spanish speakers should be presented. However, if native language is incidental to your experiment, there is no reason to include this information.

Subsection II: Apparatus (or Materials)

The second subsection of the Method section is usually called **Apparatus** or **Materials. Apparatus** is the equipment used during data collection. It might include a stopwatch, a slide projector, or a computer. **Materials** are the specific papers, computer disks, and other supplies that were prepared for the experiment. Thus, the apparatus might include a screen on which images are shown, while materials might include the answer sheet on which participants record their observations from the screen.

This subsection is not used to describe apparatus or materials used in later data analysis or manuscript preparation. **Only apparatus and materials used in data collection are described.** For example, computer software that is used for analyzing results should not be included in the method section.

The description of materials and apparatus should be brief but also complete. **Enough detail should be given that another investigator can replicate your experiment.** You should also be sure that the descriptions are clear, accurate, and free of ambiguity. In her attempt to be as concise as possible, a student once submitted a Method section that included the statement, "Time was kept with a second-hand watch." We have to assume that she meant that the time that participants took to complete the experiment was recorded in seconds, not that the psychology department could not afford a new watch!

Subsection III: Procedure

The final subsection of the Method section describes the **Procedure.** This subsection presents a complete summary of what happened in the experiment. It includes:

- Important aspects of the instructions to participant.
- How participants were assigned to conditions.
- The experimental design that was used.
- In step-by-step fashion, what the participants did.

The Procedure subsection is usually the longest and most detailed part of the Method section. It includes **identification of the specific independent and dependent variables** as well as **potential variables** that were controlled in the experiment. (If the terms **independent variable** and **dependent variable** are not familiar to you, please refer to p. 81 in Chapter 5.) This subsection also includes a description of **what participants did** during data collection.

The procedure subsection follows, in a very general way, the **inverted triangle** model of the Introduction section. The most general aspect of the procedure is usually placed first. For example, the type of experimental design that was used often leads this section. Then the specific experimental conditions are described, followed by a detailed description of what, specifically, the participants were expected to do in each of the conditions.

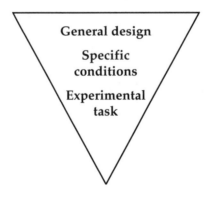

Follow chronological order when describing multiple procedures. Many experiments require the use of multiple procedures. For example, participants might first have to answer a survey designed to distinguish individual differences in familiarity with the topic of the experiment, followed by a task in which learning materials are presented and studied, followed by a memory task for the studied materials. For clarity, it is important that you describe the tasks **chronologically** when a series of procedures is involved.

Sample Method Section

On the next pages is Angela Bruflat's annotated Method section for her report on the false memory experiment. You can see that it contains all the necessary information for a reader to understand exactly what she did. Another investigator could repeat her experiment from the information presented in her introduction.

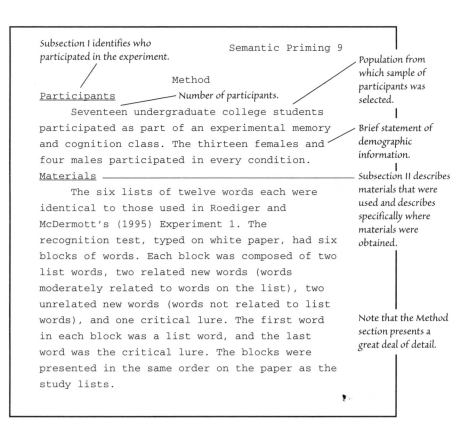

Subsection I identifies who participated in the experiment.

Semantic Priming 9

Method

Participants — *Number of participants.*

Seventeen undergraduate college students participated as part of an experimental memory and cognition class. The thirteen females and four males participated in every condition.

Materials

The six lists of twelve words each were identical to those used in Roediger and McDermott's (1995) Experiment 1. The recognition test, typed on white paper, had six blocks of words. Each block was composed of two list words, two related new words (words moderately related to words on the list), two unrelated new words (words not related to list words), and one critical lure. The first word in each block was a list word, and the last word was the critical lure. The blocks were presented in the same order on the paper as the study lists.

Population from which sample of participants was selected.

Brief statement of demographic information.

Subsection II describes materials that were used and describes specifically where materials were obtained.

Note that the Method section presents a great deal of detail.

```
                              Semantic Priming 10
```

— Subsection III.

Procedure

     Participants listened as the words were   *first*
read out loud at a rate of one word every two
seconds. Immediately after each list was read,
participants were given 45 seconds to write   *second*
down on a sheet of paper as many words as they
could remember from the list. A different sheet
of paper was used for each recall test.
Participants were instructed to write the last
few words first and then to recall the rest in
any order. They were also told to not simply
guess.

     After the last recall test, participants   *third*
were distracted from thinking about the words
by being required to attend to class
announcements. A recognition test was then
administered. Participants were instructed to   *fourth*
circle the words on the test that they
recognized from the previous presentation of
the lists. They were also instructed to mark
each word that they circled with either an R
(remember) or a K (know). The R indicated that
the participants could remember a specific
attribute of the word, such as how it sounded
as it was pronounced. The K signified that the
participant felt certain that the word was on
the list but could not recall any specific
details about it.

Note that procedures are described chronologically:

SECTION 5: RESULTS

The **Results** section summarizes the statistical outcome of your experiment. In this section, you should present all relevant descriptive and inferential statistics. Please note that while this section does not address your hypotheses specifically, the statistics that are used should be appropriate for evaluating them.

This section is also where tables and figures that show the study's results are used. **Tables** present exact values of means, correlations, probabilities, and so on in an easily understood structure. Tables are better than figures for showing precise outcomes. They can summarize your descriptive statistics (for example, means and standard deviations for each condition in your experiment) or present a list of inferential statistical results that would be unwieldy if presented in the text.

Sample Table

TABLE 1   Mean Number of Correct Responses on First, Second, and Third Tasks

Task	Age of Children				
	5	7	9	11	13
First	8.7	10.2	10.8	10.9	14.8
Second	10.0	15.8	18.0	18.9	20.9
Third	9.5	16.0	17.7	23.8	23.9

Figures present a graphical display of statistical outcomes. Figures are often used to show trends in results or to display statistical interactions between two or more variables. Several kinds of figures are commonly used. **Frequency polygons** are line graphs; points that show the location on the Y-axis for each score on X are connected. Frequency polygons are often used when the values tested come from a **continuous variable**—that is, when the variable has a continuum of scores that could have been tested between those on the figure. The line connecting the points is assumed to estimate intermediate values between those being tested. A frequency polygon implies that these values exist. For example, if the independent variable is time, and the levels tested are 1, 2, and 3 hours, these values represent only three of an infinite number of available times that could have been chosen for the experiment, and the point on the line midway between the 1- and 2-hour scores is considered to be an estimate of participants' performance at the 1½-hour duration. On the other hand, if religious preference were the independent variable being tested and people who identified themselves as Muslim, Jewish, Hindu, and Christian were selected, a frequency polygon would not be appropriate for representing results in a figure because there is no identifiable "religion" between any two of the four that were investigated.

When the variable being tested is **discrete**—that is, when no identifiable levels exist between those being tested—**bar graphs** should be used when depicting results in figures. **Bar graphs** are figures that show research results by a series of (usually vertical) bars. Bars on a bar graph do not touch each other, suggesting that intermediate points do not exist. The religion example in the last paragraph illustrates a discrete variable. There is no continuum of recognized religions that forms a continuous and infinite number of possible levels.

Histograms are bar graphs in which adjacent bars touch each other. This type of figure may be used in place of a frequency polygon when results can be better depicted by bars than by lines. Because each bar in a histogram touches the adjacent bars, this type of figure is assumed to represent a continuous variable. More detail about figures and tables and their use can be found in almost any statistics or research design book.

Location of Tables and Figures in a Lab Report

While tables and figures usually refer to research results and their placement in a **published** manuscript is usually in the Results section, they are placed at the end of the manuscript in its **word-processed** form. Each table and figure is placed on a separate page and appears after the Reference section. Tables and figures are numbered consecutively in the order in which they appear in the text. A table caption appears above the table itself. However, since figures are often prepared on glossy paper, their captions appear on separate pages.

When Should a Table or Figure Be Used?

Writers of experimental laboratory reports must make their own decisions about whether numerical results should be included in the text of the Results section or stand by themselves in a table or a figure.

A general rule of thumb is that if only a few numbers need to be presented, and these numbers form a string of results representing only one independent variable, they should be included in the text. However, if there is a long series of numbers, or if the numbers represent scores or results from two or more variables, a table or figure is usually clearer. Thus, if an experiment includes only three conditions and the means and standard deviations of these conditions are reported, a separate table or figure is not warranted. However, if the experimental design includes two or more different independent variables with several levels of each, readers will be able to make more sense of the results if means and standard deviations are presented in a table or figure.

Other Points to Remember in Formatting Your Results

Identify Figures and Tables in the Text
When you write a Results section, there are several important points to keep in mind. First, tables and figures must be referred to in the text of this section; they cannot stand by themselves. For example, in your text you might state, "Mean judgments of familiarity across age and education levels are shown in Figure 1." However, it would not be appropriate to include that figure without identifying it in the text of the results section.

Include Descriptive Statistics to Support Inferential Statistics
Second, whenever an inferential statistic (that is, a statistic that relates the outcome to the general population) is reported, the relevant descriptive statistic (that is, the summary statistic of the results of your experiment) must be included as well. Using the example in the last paragraph, if differences in mean judgment scores for familiarity are statistically significant, the mean of each of the familiarity judgment conditions must be identified in the text or in a figure or table.

Avoid Redundancy
Third, the same information should *not* be presented in several formats. This means that if mean scores are presented in the text, they should not be presented in a table or figure as well. In a similar vein, tables and figures should not include the same information. In other words, APA style requires a minimum of redundancy in its manuscripts. The rationale for this requirement is the same as that for limiting the extent of the literature review in the introduction: research reports must be succinct and compact.

Don't Use the Results Section for "Discussion" Text
Finally, the Results section is *not* the place to discuss statistical outcomes with reference to your hypotheses. This section simply presents the outcomes that you obtained. Conclusions that you draw from the results are reserved for the Discussion section.

Sample Results Section

Now it is time for Angela Bruflat's Results section. As you may remember, she completed an experiment investigating false memory by having participants listen to a series of six lists of related words with twelve words in each. After each list was heard, participants had to attempt to recall the words in the list. After all the lists had been presented and a recall test had been administered after each, six recognition tests—each consisting of two correct list words, two related new words, two unrelated new words and the critical lure—were administered.

Because this experiment was completed in the laboratory section of an experimental course in memory and cognition, only the recognition test results were analyzed, and this analysis only included overall means and standard deviations and a general analysis of variance. The recall results were ignored. Thus, this Results section is not as complete as one that might appear in a journal publication or that a student might prepare for an individual research project. However, it is probably comparable to the level of detail that you will be writing in an undergraduate experimental laboratory course.

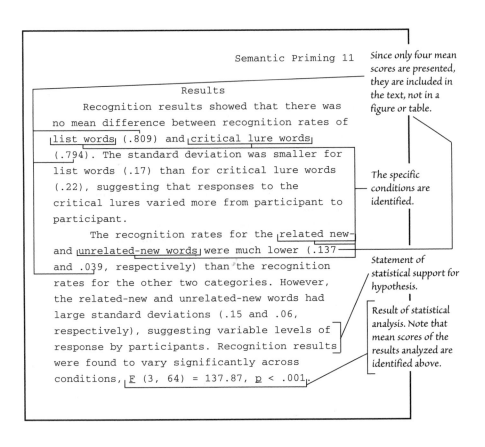

Semantic Priming 11

Since only four mean scores are presented, they are included in the text, not in a figure or table.

Results

Recognition results showed that there was no mean difference between recognition rates of list words (.809) and critical lure words (.794). The standard deviation was smaller for list words (.17) than for critical lure words (.22), suggesting that responses to the critical lures varied more from participant to participant.

The specific conditions are identified.

The recognition rates for the related new and unrelated-new words were much lower (.137 and .039, respectively) than the recognition rates for the other two categories. However, the related-new and unrelated-new words had large standard deviations (.15 and .06, respectively), suggesting variable levels of response by participants. Recognition results were found to vary significantly across conditions, $F(3, 64) = 137.87$, $p < .001$.

Statement of statistical support for hypothesis.

Result of statistical analysis. Note that mean scores of the results analyzed are identified above.

SECTION 6: DISCUSSION

The **Discussion** section is where you **interpret** your statistics and present their **implications** within the context of your hypotheses. As with the Introduction, there is a conventional substructure to the Discussion. In the first paragraph or two, it is common to **evaluate your hypotheses. Did the results of your experiment support them? If so, how?** The beginning of the Discussion section is often simply a statement of support or nonsupport of the hypotheses you stated in the Introduction.

In the middle paragraphs, you will **compare your results** with those of others and **draw inferences** from these comparisons. Most of the studies that you reference in the Discussion should have already been described in the Introduction to your paper. The middle paragraphs of the Discussion are where researchers commonly explain in detail their conclusions and the bases for making them.

This is also where unexpected or unpredicted results are discussed. If you obtained such a result, you may be able to explain it on the basis of a characteristic of your experimental design or the particular sample of participants you used. *However, it is not the place to be defensive.* Perhaps an unpredicted outcome occurred because your hypothesis was wrong! As in the Introduction, take care to avoid personal attacks and arguments that are not substantiated by the outcome of the experiment.

The final part of the discussion usually includes **statements about possible shortcomings** of the experiment and **directions for future research.** These final paragraphs might point out additional variables that should be studied for a more complete understanding of the issue at hand. They also may identify potential **practical applications** of the research.

Because of its complexity, the Discussion section often appears to be the most difficult section of an experimental paper to write. But for a researcher who has carefully reviewed the literature about the topic at hand and who has developed and tested a set of well thought-out hypotheses, the discussion presents an opportunity to tie all the parts of the report together. Here the investigator can demonstrate the importance of the study in the context of the problem that he or she investigated.

Sample Discussion Section

Angela Bruflat's annotated Discussion section is now presented. Her results showed that participants falsely recognized critical lures at about the same rate as they correctly recognized words that had been presented in the lists of words that they heard. However, other related and unrelated words were not falsely recognized to any extent. Now Angela will attempt to explain these results in the context of her hypotheses and previous studies of false memory.

Semantic Priming 12

Discussion

Results support the initial hypothesis that
the critical lures will have higher recognition
rates than other new words and a recognition
rate that is similar to old words. We can be
fairly confident that the design used in this
experiment is a reliable one. Roediger and
McDermott (1995) used a similar design with
comparable participants and found the same
results. The same basic design with minor
manipulations yielded the same results in
several other studies as well (McDermott, 1996;
Payne et al., 1996; Read, 1996).

First paragraph: interpret the statistical outcome— refer to hypotheses identified in the Introduction.

In line with previous research, these
results fit into the framework of a semantic
activation model. This experiment can be
viewed as a semantic priming experiment (Meyer
& Schvaneveldt, 1971). This model proposes that
activation of one concept primes another, that
is, it leads to a greater likelihood that
related concepts will be activated. According
to the spreading activation model, the more
properties that concepts share, the more links
there should be between the nodes representing
the concepts and properties (Collins & Loftus,
1975). Thus, if numerous related words are
presented which all strongly relate to another
word (that is, the critical lure) other primed
words are likely to be activated.

Relate interpretation to previous research.

However, there are several threats to the
validity of this experiment. First, the use of
college students as participants is
particularly questionable. College students not
only focus much of their energy on memorizing
material, but they are likely to have developed
systems for chunking (combining several pieces
of information into one large unit) and

Statement of possible shortcomings.

Semantic Priming 13

determining major themes of word lists. This could have systematically affected the recognition test and at least be responsible for more robust results than might have been expected with a more representative sample. This possibility may be even more pronounced in this particular experiment, as well as in Roediger and McDermott's (1995), because participants were enrolled in memory and cognition classes. These classes are fairly advanced undergraduate classes, and the students in them have made it to that point in their education by, in part, being especially successful and adept at memorization and drawing main points from studied material.

Again, relate (in this case, possible shortcomings) to previous research.

Another potential threat to the validity of this experiment is due to the fact that several students arrived late, after the directions and the first word of the first list were read aloud. The directions were repeated, so some participants had double exposure to the first word. On one hand, this does not seem especially threatening since only the first word was involved. According to the well-supported primacy effect, the first few words of a list, especially the very first, are the most likely to be remembered. However, in light of the spreading activation model (Collins & Loftus, 1975), the first word may have been activated more strongly, leading to a stronger trace and a larger amount of spreading in associated areas of the network.

There is also the question of whether the results would be different if a recall test were not administered prior to the recognition test. Based on previous research, it is likely that the act of recalling enhances subsequent

Connects closely to information in Introduction.

```
                              Semantic Priming 14

recognition of both studied items and the
critical lures (Roediger & McDermott, 1995;
McDermott, 1996).
     While this experiment and other similar
ones offer evidence for the existence of false
memories, extreme caution should be exercised
in generalizing these findings to the current
controversy regarding recovered memories of
child abuse. As pointed out by Freyd and
Gleaves (1996), this type of experiment is
really testing memory for specific items or
objects (words), not actual events or episodes
(the entire memory of participating in the
experiment). Freyd and Gleaves also argue that
it is not appropriate to generalize research
findings such as these to events as dissimilar
as child abuse.
```

Discussion of limits on generalizability.

NOW IT IS TIME TO WRITE SECTION 2: ABSTRACT

The **Abstract** is discussed last among the textual parts of the paper because it is the last section you will write. Although it appears at the front of the paper in print, the Abstract provides a brief summary of the entire work, and it should be written after all the other parts have been essentially completed.

Since the Abstract is essentially a concise summary of the entire paper, it usually makes little sense to draft it before the rest of the text is done. As Chapters 2 and 3 describe, writing is a process that involves continual revision. Often, new ideas and slants for repositioning parts of the report occur during the predrafting and drafting of the main body of the paper. If the Abstract is meant to summarize the paper, waiting until the rest of the paper is essentially written can save a great deal of writing time and effort in preparing the Abstract.

In a way, the Abstract is the most important section of a paper. For reports that appear in journals, the Abstract is the section that will be read by the most people. It normally appears unedited in printed form in

Psychological Abstracts and in electronic form in *PsycINFO* and *PsycLIT*. It is the section of the report that will determine whether the remainder appears important to a reader. Thus, a well-written abstract can increase readership.

The abstract of an empirical study must inform the reader of the:

- **Research question**
- **Participants** (including how many were used)
- **Method** used to investigate the problem
- **Results**
- **Conclusions**

Normally, this information is presented in the order in which it appears in the body of the paper. Thus, the Abstract presents a brief overview of the Introduction, Method, Results, and Discussion sections, respectively.

An Abstract must be very concise. It is normally limited to about 100–120 words. In that limited space, a writer must capture the reason for conducting the study, the methodology used, and the conclusions drawn. Thus, **brevity** and **conciseness** are at a premium.

Tips for Writing Abstracts

Writers can be both complete and concise by using a number of tricks of the trade. First, **limit the number of function words:** that is, do not use any more articles, conjunctions, prepositions, or other superfluous words than necessary. The article *the* is always a good candidate for omission. For example, "The results showed . . ." loses nothing if *the* is omitted.

Second, **use active voice.** It is more efficient and more forceful to say, "Results showed . . ." than "It was found that. . . ."

Third, **make liberal use of clauses and phrases.** The basis for running your experiment may be able to be summarized by the phrase "to determine whether imagery has an influence on recall." The sentence "The intent of the experiment was to determine whether imagery has an influence on recall" wastes words.

Avoiding Confusion in the Abstract

Because the Abstract must stand alone and may be read by people who will not read the rest of the article, it is important to remember that abbreviations and unique or idiosyncratic terms that you may have used in the body of the paper cannot be used in the Abstract. All abbreviations and acronyms must be either omitted or defined in the Abstract itself.

By all accounts, the Abstract contains the most information in the fewest number of words of any section of an experimental report. Therefore, it is critical that the writing be crisp and focused. Writers of good Abstracts are able to state all essential information and omit all nonessential information.

Editing the Abstract

A useful exercise after drafting an Abstract is to edit it in two steps. First, see if some of the articles (*as, ans,* and *thes*) and other function words can be deleted without compromising the flow of the text. Then see if the text can be shortened by presenting the information contained in some of the sentences as prepositional phrases and relative clauses. Most writers find that length can be reduced by at least 10 percent by these two steps.

Sample Abstract

Angela Bruflat's annotated Abstract in her report of her experiment on false memory demonstrates how an Abstract must be complete yet very concise. The gist of the basis for running the experiment, the methodology, the results, and the conclusions are all captured in just a few sentences. Please note that the Abstract always appears on page 2 of a laboratory paper. Here is Angela's Abstract.

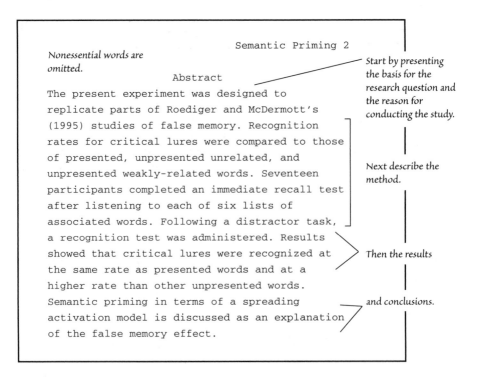

Semantic Priming 2

Nonessential words are omitted.

Abstract

The present experiment was designed to replicate parts of Roediger and McDermott's (1995) studies of false memory. Recognition rates for critical lures were compared to those of presented, unpresented unrelated, and unpresented weakly-related words. Seventeen participants completed an immediate recall test after listening to each of six lists of associated words. Following a distractor task, a recognition test was administered. Results showed that critical lures were recognized at the same rate as presented words and at a higher rate than other unpresented words. Semantic priming in terms of a spreading activation model is discussed as an explanation of the false memory effect.

Start by presenting the basis for the research question and the reason for conducting the study.

Next describe the method.

Then the results

and conclusions.

SECTION 7: REFERENCES

Because Chapter 8 presents a guide to correct APA citation and an extensive bibliography that employs APA citation style and format, details of constructing a **Reference** section will not be reviewed here. However, three important points about references in APA experimental laboratory reports should be emphasized.

First, **the references listed in the Reference section must match exactly the ones identified in the text.** Unlike a bibliography, which may be mandated by some other writing styles, a Reference section does not include mention of articles and books that might be of interest to the reader but that are not included in the text of the article. This means that in preparing manuscripts, researchers frequently read far more source materials than are listed.

Second, **only sources that you actually used in your literature search should be included in the text and in the Reference section.** This means that if you accessed a secondary source, that source, not the primary book or article, should be referenced. It is never appropriate to report a study by Smith (1986) if you read about Smith's study in Jones (1997). Only Jones (1997) should be cited. Every instructor of an experimental psychology lab course can cite cases where students have included references to books long out of print or articles in a language that the student does not speak because the student reported an unread primary source.

Finally, **experimental reports do not include exhaustive reviews of prior research completed on a topic.** Instead, if a review exists, you may include mention of it in the text and the Reference section and direct readers to refer to that article.

Sample Reference Section

We conclude our presentation of Angela Bruflat's paper with her Reference section. Please note that the Reference section always begins on a new page and that like all other sections of a manuscript written in APA format, it is double spaced throughout. All the references in Angela's text are included in this section, and no references in this section are not included in the text.

References

Alba, J. W., & Hasher, L. (1983). Is memory schematic? Psychological Bulletin, 93, 203-231.

Bartlett, F. C. (1932). Remembering: A study in experimental and social psychology. Cambridge, England: Cambridge University Press.

Brainerd, C. J., & Reyna, V. F. (1990). Gist is the grist: Fuzzy-trace theory and new intuitionism. Developmental Review, 10, 3-47.

Bransford, J. D., & Franks, J. J. (1971). The abstraction of linguistic ideas. Cognitive Psychology, 2, 331-350.

Collins, A. M., & Loftus, E. F. (1975). A spreading activation theory of semantic processing. Psychological Review, 82, 407-428.

Freyd, J. J., & Gleaves, D. H. (1996). "Remembering" words not presented in lists: Relevance to the current recovered/false memory controversy. Journal of Experimental Psychology: Learning, Memory, and Cognition, 22, 811-813.

McDermott, K. B. (1996). The persistence of false memories in list recall. Journal of Memory and Language, 35, 212-230.

Meyer, D. E., & Schvaneveldt, R. W. (1971). Facilitation in recognizing pairs of words: Evidence of a dependence between retrieval operations. Journal of Experimental Psychology, 90, 227-234.

Payne, D. G., Elie, C. J., Blackwell, J. M., & Neuschatz, J. S. (1996). Memory illusions: Recalling, recognizing, and recollecting events that never occurred. Journal of Memory and Language, 35, 261-285.

Read, J. D. (1996). From a passing thought to a false memory in two minutes: Confusing

References in the text match exactly those in the Reference section.

References are presented in APA format: see Chapter 8.

Like all parts of the lab report, references are double spaced.

Semantic Priming 16

real and illusory events. <u>Psychonomic Bulletin</u> <u>and Review, 3,</u> 105-111.

    Roediger, H. L. III, & McDermott, K. B. (1995). Creating false memories: Remembering words not presented in lists. <u>Journal of</u> <u>Experimental Psychology: Learning, Memory and</u> <u>Cognition, 21,</u> 803-814.

FINALLY . . . TRY TO TELL A STORY ABOUT SOLVING A PROBLEM

A useful way to think about the overall report is as a story that you are telling. The story starts, at the beginning of the Introduction section, with identification of a problem that needs to be addressed. The problem is then discussed later in the Introduction in terms of how other people have dealt with it. The Introduction ends with the investigator's proposed solution to the problem.

The second part of the story, presented in the Method section, describes the specific details of the investigator's attempts to solve the problem. Part 3 presents the Results of this attempt, and Part 4, found in the Discussion section, explains and evaluates these results in terms of the original problem and the previous attempts to solve it. Thus, the entire manuscript is connected around the problem and its solution; the story has a defined plot, attempted solution, and outcome.

While an experimental report is divided into defined sections, each with its own heading, **the story it tells must hang together.** No part of it stands alone, independent of other parts. The best writers of experimental reports are those who write so that no loose ends are dangling and all parts make sense within the whole.

5

WRITING TERM PAPERS AND CRITICAL EVALUATIONS OF RESEARCH PAPERS

If you are a student whose major is psychology, or if you are enrolled in upper-level psychology classes, you will almost certainly have any number of papers to write that are not part of a laboratory assignment (covered in Chapter 4). Some of these will require that you read and review articles in psychology journals and book chapters and critically evaluate their content. Others will require that you write about a broader topic, often integrating information from several sources into a focused and coherent paper that both informs the reader and evaluates the topic and the research related to it.

The type of writing to be discussed in this chapter deals with these types of papers. The writing **explains** the topics and methods used in the articles and chapters, **summarizes** their conclusions, critically **evaluates** the research, and, often, **suggests new directions** for later research. Unlike laboratory reports, this writing does not describe empirical research that you have personally done. Instead, it presents a summary and critical review of a single article or a number of articles dealing with a research topic.

In general, you will find two kinds of writing assignments of this type. The first is a fairly **short critical review** (for example, 4–6 pages) of a published research article. The second is a **longer review of a relatively specific topic area, theory, or integrated body of research.** The second type of paper is usually called a **term paper** (and we will use that name as well), a name that comes from the fact that it is usually a major assignment over the duration of a college *term*. (You might note that it is usually assigned fairly early in the term, to allow time for research and writing—in other words, engaging in the complete writing process. It is wise not to treat this assignment as an "end-of-term" paper, but to allow time for last minute catastrophes—computer crashes, library access problems, etc.—as well as opportunities for peer review and last-minute editorial changes!)

Writing these two types of papers is presented in the same chapter because they are similar in many ways, and many of the suggestions and recommendations you will read here apply to both. This chapter will first discuss shorter critical reviews of single research articles and follow up with discussion of lengthier term papers, but we think you will find important points in each section, regardless of the type of paper you are writing.

But first, a caveat. You may find that some of your term paper assignments in psychology classes don't emphasize critical evaluation of psychological research. They may require more summary and description than evaluation, or they may include summaries of your personal experiences— for example, at service learning or practicum sites. However, you should keep in mind that psychology's database has been established through empirical research. The topics you are describing and the experiences you are summarizing have come into existence as a result of scientists doing their work. Grades on very few term papers will be lowered because a student included a well-reasoned and well-documented critical review.

WRITING CRITICAL REVIEWS

"Choose any article published in the last five years in one of the following journals, and write a 4–6 page critical review of it. In your review, be sure to summarize the article and present a concise evaluation of (a) the development of the hypothesis, (b) the method used to test the hypothesis, and (c) the conclusions that the investigator drew."

The previous paragraph, followed by a short list of journal titles from which an article can be selected, presents typical wording for an assignment that many students, at least initially, have come to dread! If an article has already appeared in print, it has probably already been reviewed by one or more experts and found to pass muster. How could an instructor possibly feel that a lowly student could provide a worthwhile evaluation?

Critical Reviews as Professional Preparation

This assignment can be very valuable for students in many ways. For students who plan on attending graduate school in psychology or who have aspirations of a research career, evaluating psychological literature will be a continuing professional activity.

This assignment can also hone critical thinking and analytic skills that will transfer to many important professional situations. The best graduate schools and the best research labs really like letters of recommendation that include statements such as "This student is creative in proposing research studies," or "This student can synthesize information from diverse topics." Being creative in a research setting means being able to develop research hypotheses and deduce ways to appropriately test them. Evaluating the hypotheses and procedures used by others is an excellent way to develop these creative research skills. "Synthesizing information from diverse topics" means being able to make connections among findings from several different areas of research to see potential applications of these connections. When you begin to critically evaluate prior research studies, you are essentially learning to do an important task that may become part of your professional life for years to come.

Before discussing this type of learning, let's take a few moments to talk about **theories, models,** and **hypotheses.**

Theories, for psychologists, are sets of assumptions that connect existing data and relate research findings. They are also used for making predictions about new data. Theories are usually fairly broad, encompassing a large number of prior findings and possible future research results.

Models are sometimes used synonymously with theories, but they usually have a logical, quantitative, or physical basis. Models are often *analogs* or *metaphors* on which we base our understanding of psychological principles. For example, a stage model of memory that includes sensory memory, working memory, and long-term memory as sequential stages in the processing of information presents us with a structure for organizing research on memory.

Hypotheses are derived from theories and models. They are the specific research predictions that emerge from theories and models and from research already completed. A hypothesis identifies an outcome that a researcher hopes or expects to obtain. Students who have studied hypothesis testing in statistics classes will recognize this as a statement of the **alternative** (sometimes called the **experimental**) **hypothesis.** The **alternative hypothesis** is essentially the researcher's hypothesis as it is applied to statistics. If the hypothesis is affirmed statistically, it means that the research results supported the hypothesis the investigator stated.

Why did we take this little diversion into some of the concepts of psychological research? Because the type of writing described in this chapter usually involves critical reviews of empirical research, and a top-of-the-line paper must demonstrate that the student knows how research works. One of the surest ways to earn an A on such a paper is to point out the things that the investigator did well and didn't do well in relating research to theory.

Now let's discuss some points to think about in writing such a paper.

What a Critical Review Should Contain

A critical review should include both (1) a **brief summary** of the article being reviewed, and (2) a **critique** of at least some parts of it. The **summary** should include the:

- **Purpose of the research**
- **Hypothesis or hypotheses** of the investigator
- **Method** the investigator used
- **Results** obtained
- **Conclusions** that were drawn

The reason for including this much information in your summary is that all these aspects of a research paper are fair grounds for criticism. A good critical review evaluates at least some of these points.

The **critique** should be a logical, well-formed evaluation of most of the parts of the paper that were just identified. Later in this chapter, we'll point out some aspects of each of these parts that you might look for in your critique. However, it is important to remember that your criticisms must be grounded in logic and knowledge of study design and relevant theory. They must not be capricious or personal.

1. Writing the Summary
In order to make your critique meaningful to a reader, you must present enough detail about the study to allow the reader to make sense of your analysis. Unless sufficient detail about what the investigator did is presented, your evaluation will not make much sense to the reader.

Describing Purpose and Hypotheses.   Every published study describes a reason (or two, or three, or more) why the research was undertaken in the first place. Usually the reason is to test a hypothesis generated from a more general theory—hence the reason for discussing hypotheses and theories. The purpose behind the study is always found in the **Introduction** section of a research article, and it usually appears near the end of this section. (See Chapter 4 for a description of the parts and general organization of a research study.)

Through the beginning and middle portions of an Introduction section of a research article, most well-written papers present an overview of the theory or model that formed the basis of the research and results of some related prior studies. From this, the investigator's hypothesis is generated. As you are writing your review, you should pay particular attention to the *relationship* between the *purpose* of the research, within the context of the theory or model, and the *specific predictions* of the investigator. Good reviews should include evaluative comments on the soundness of this relationship. Therefore, you should describe this aspect of the article you are reviewing in some detail.

Another caveat: It is not true that all psychological research is theoretically based. While most of the studies you read will present theories or models which underlie them, there are other bases for research as well. Some research is designed to investigate new applications of existing knowledge. Some of it is designed to simply replicate earlier research (that is, repeat an earlier study) and validate its findings. But every study must have some basis for its existence. Whatever it is (according to the investigator), you should be sure to describe it in your summary of the article.

Describing the Method.   Your review should include enough information about the method used by the investigator to allow your reader (usually your instructor) to **understand the basic procedure** that was used and to **discern the bases for any criticisms** that you might have. It is especially important to describe the independent and dependent variables (see p. 81) because they must be relevant to the research question being investigated. However, it is not usually necessary to go into a great deal of detail on all aspects of the methods that the investigator used. Generally, you should identify the types of people (college students, business executives, whatever)—or perhaps animals—who participated, and briefly discuss the general design and procedure of the study. Unlike a summary of your own research, in which you must present enough detail to enable another investigator to reproduce your study (see Chapter 4), if you are reviewing the work of another, all that is necessary is that you present sufficient detail so that the reader can understand what was done and see the bases for your criticisms.

Summarizing Results.   Your summary of the study's results is usually brief. After all, assuming that data collection and statistical outcomes were reported accurately, there is seldom much to evaluate in this section of the paper. About the only exception to brevity in your results summary would occur if you can suggest suitable ways of improving the types of measurements or statistical analyses that were performed. For example, if you can present a way that the study might be improved by using a different type of statistical analysis, you should certainly describe in some detail the statistics that the investigator used.

Describing the Conclusions.   You should give a rather detailed account of the study's conclusions, especially as they relate to the hypothesis or other basis for doing the research that you described earlier. You should also be aware of any limitations that the investigator placed on the conclusions. That is, did the article indicate that the conclusions are valid only with certain populations or only within certain constraints imposed by the study? When we discuss the evaluation of the study, we will present some things to look for that often form the basis for critical evaluation, so ensuring that your readers know what the investigator concluded from the results is important.

General Rule of Thumb.   When you are summarizing a study that forms the basis for your critical evaluation, be sure to present a good deal of detail on the parts you are going to address in your evaluation. As with all papers (including those not written for psychology courses), all parts must hang together. A critical evaluation, whether it is positive or negative, doesn't make much sense unless the reader is also presented with the grounds for the evaluation.

2. Writing the Critique

The description of the research study provides the groundwork for the evaluation itself. You have by now completed the **summary** of the article and it is time to present your analysis and criticism. The remainder of this section of the chapter will identify some of the most common **critical questions** of a study that you should attend to in your analysis.

   a. **Is the purpose clearly stated, and does it relate to the underlying theory or to other bases for research described in the study's introduction?** The reason for paying close attention to the investigator's development of the purpose of the study is to see if there exists a reasonable and valid basis for conducting the research. The study should be designed to fill in a gap in our knowledge or to extend our knowledge to new populations or to a wider range of situations. Perhaps the study was designed to evaluate a theory, to compare predictions of competing theories, or to demonstrate an application of a psychological phenomenon. Whatever the purpose of the research, it should emerge *logically* and *clearly* in the introduction, and its value should be apparent.

   b. **Does the hypothesis make sense in the context of the theory or model from which it was developed?** Remember that the hypothesis is the specific prediction that the investigator makes. It predicts a certain behavioral outcome for the study's participants. As such, the behavior should fit the purpose of the study. In experimental psychology terms, the **independent variable** (that is, the variable that is intentionally manipulated by the investigator in an experiment) must be appropriate for the predictions of the model or theory. Also, the **dependent variable** (that is, the specific behavioral measure used to assess the effects of the independent variable) must measure an appropriate behavior. *Example:* Let us say that the theory predicts that adolescents should show more emotion in a situation that is personally relevant than in one that isn't. In this study, the investigator should choose a dependent variable that allows differential degrees of emotion to be measured (e.g., facial expression or heart rate) and an independent variable that clearly differentiates personally relevant from impersonal situations.

c. **Have a reasonable number of participants been tested?** These next few paragraphs are for the (moderately) statistically sophisticated! We are going to discuss things like **sample size, effect size,** and **statistical power.** If you have completed a statistics course (and most psychology majors must do this sometime in their college careers) you should be aware of these concepts. **Statistical power** is a measure of the likelihood that an investigator will find statistical support for his or her hypothesis, given that the effect is real. One way to increase statistical power is to increase sample size—that is, to use more participants in the study. As the number of participants in a research study increases, the more likely it is that the research hypothesis will be statistically supported.

However, this doesn't always mean that a very large sample should be used. If a hypothesized outcome requires a very large amount of data in order to achieve statistical significance, it implies that the independent variable is not very potent—that is, it has only a minor effect in producing differences in performance. *Example:* Suppose that in the overall population a very slight difference between men's and women's performance exists for a given independent variable (let's say that if the entire population could be measured, women would show an effect 60.5% of the time and men would show an effect 60.8% of the time). A study that used only a small sample of men and women would be unlikely to detect this difference; a very large number of participants would be necessary. However, the very fact that so many measurements had to be made suggests that the effect is very small and probably not very important in understanding sex differences.

Thus, there is a tradeoff between the size of real-world effects and the amount of data that must be collected. Statisticians have pointed out that there is probably a difference, however minuscule, between almost every possible population on almost every possible variable that can be measured. But who cares! If it takes a cast of thousands to demonstrate that, say, women in a particular organization have an IQ that is two-tenths of a point higher than that of men, the result is trivial when it comes to generating organizational policies.

But there is another side to this complicated picture. If only a few scores are collected, a result that fails to support the investigator's hypothesis may be overlooking potentially important outcomes. A study in which only a few scores are measured may lack the statistical power to support the investigator's hypothesis, even if the effect is fairly large.

Fortunately, the fourth edition of the *Publication Manual of the American Psychological Association* has some suggestions for dealing with this dilemma. The manual suggests that statistical power and effect size be addressed when reporting statistical outcomes. (Earlier editions of the manual, however, were generally silent on these factors, so articles published before 1995 or 1996 did not usually report them.) Therefore, you can get an idea not only of the statistical reliability of the study's outcome, but of the potential size of it as well.

d. Do participants represent an appropriate population for the study being reported? All psychologists who report studies in psychological journals are interested in their outcomes' relevance to far more individuals than those participants whom they tested. As you have become aware in almost every psychology course you have completed, psychologists almost always deal with **samples,** smaller subsets of individuals from larger **populations.** The populations are the groups that are really important in research. Few psychologists would pay attention to research findings if conclusions were limited to the small number of participants included in the study being reported. The real key to research is whether conclusions extend beyond the people actually tested. This, of course, is why we have inferential statistics.

But when a result turns out to be statistically significant, sampling theory says that it can only be generalized to the population from which the sample was selected. Thus, results from a sample of 5-year-old children, if statistically significant, can generalize only to the population of 5-year-old children, not to other populations.

Sampling theory has caused psychologists some discomfort. Most studies in psychology have used college students as participants, and a strong case can be made that the population of college students is not the sole group that the results of many studies have been applied to. Indeed, a wag wrote once that psychology now knows all there is to know about college sophomores and white rats! The reasons, of course, for our reliance on these populations is that most samples in psychological research are selected for the convenience of the investigator. College sophomores (and freshmen and juniors and seniors) and white rats are readily available. College students who are enrolled in psychology classes often have built-in class incentives for participating. As for white rats? Among their best traits is that they never fail to show up at the appointed place and time when they are "signed up" to participate!

Normally, psychologists don't feel that limiting participants to these populations presents too much of a problem, at least where basic research is concerned. They generally agree that findings of behavioral and cognitive properties of college sophomores are probably still pretty valid despite the narrow parameters of the samples that are used. But some research, especially if it is targeting specific populations, should use samples taken from those populations. A study that is interested in leadership styles of CEOs of major business organizations is certainly more valid if CEOs actually participate. And certainly, if children of different age ranges are predicted to perform differently, children serving as participants must represent those ranges.

e. Were the study design and the procedures used in the investigation appropriate? Evaluation of this part of a research paper can be tricky. There is usually plenty of disagreement among psychologists regarding the best design to use in investigating various phenomena. But there are certain things you can look for.

Psychology uses many approaches to research, including experimentation, correlational studies, case studies, and naturalistic observation. Was the right approach used? For example, if an investigator wanted to identify the cause of a particular behavior, did he or she use an experimental approach? How valid is a case study in its generalizability to other people in similar situations?

f. Were the conclusions appropriate for the results that were obtained? This question relates to what the investigator determined from the outcome of the study. Did the conclusions follow from the statistical results? Or did the investigator speculate too much about why results that didn't support the hypothesis were obtained?

g. What about generalizability of the study? As discussed, there is almost no research in psychology that is designed to relate only to the sample of people that participated, the specific levels of the independent variable tested, or the specific dependent variable that was used. Psychologists are always interested in the larger population, a wider range of possible factors that might influence behavior, and a wider range of behaviors than those tested. For example, a psychologist who surveys management styles of 50 upper-level managers is nearly always interested in upper-level management style in general.

It is frequently the case that generalizability is an important issue in evaluation of research papers. You may identify topics or populations that are relevant to the research that the investigator has not reported. Or, on the other hand, you may perceive limitations in the generalizability of the research because of a restricted range of participants, a limitation of the study design, or some other factor.

h. What are possible applications? Some studies in psychology have their basis in applying knowledge to new or different situations. These studies are often not driven by theory, but rather by the desire to apply information that has already been well established by earlier research. *Example:* It is well known that some of the myriad problems that caused the radioactive leakage at the Three Mile Island nuclear generating facility had their roots in displays and controls that were not designed to enable humans to use them accurately and quickly. The failure to take human factors into account adequately in the design of the Three Mile Island facility has led to extensive research in applying psychological principles in the redesign of control panels and visual displays to allow faster and more accurate responses in high-tech environments.

In describing an **applied research study,** the investigator should clearly state how his or her results might affect the way we deal with the world. This description is often the most important part of an applied study, and the investigator's description is one point that a critical review often addresses.

- Did the investigator identify realistic applications of the findings, or were the proposed applications based on shaky empirical grounds?
- Was the application sufficiently broad to have meaningful consequences? Or was it too broad or not broad enough?
- Were there other potential related applications that were not addressed, or not sufficiently addressed, in the paper?

Any or all of these questions can provide a basis for evaluation of an applications research report.

Identifying Potential Applications.   You should also note that there is nothing wrong with identifying potential applications of results of studies that were not specifically designed for this purpose. Often, an individual who is familiar with an area of psychology that was not the focus of a research project can apply the finding in this new area. *Example:* Behavior therapy would never have developed without extensive research in classical and operant conditioning, but the early behaviorists who did many of these investigations were certainly not primarily interested in clinical applications of their work.

Summary

We have presented some suggestions for reviewing and evaluating research articles written by other psychologists. While such an exercise may appear daunting, reviews such as these are an essential part of the professional activities of all researchers. They also incorporate a number of writing techniques to increase learning and understanding (see Chapter 2). As psychology students, as well as professionals in the discipline, develop their critical reading skills, they will also develop insight into how psychology has developed its database.

WRITING TERM PAPERS

"Choose a topic, model, or theory related to the material discussed in this course and submit a 12–15 page paper which summarizes and critically evaluates recent research related to it. Be sure that your paper includes up-to-date references and that it presents both an overview and critical evaluation of your topic. The paper is due one week before the last day of class. Be sure to clear your topic with me by the date of the midterm exam."

This assignment is sometimes accompanied by a sample list of topics, or, perhaps, by a list from which the paper topic must be chosen. It also may require, or allow the option of, multiple drafts, with the instructor reviewing and commenting on early drafts of the paper. (See Chapter 3 for advice on effective handling of this process of drafting and revision.)

It is nearly impossible to graduate from college without writing term papers. And term papers in psychology are like term papers in other disciplines in many ways. In all disciplines, each student must (1) choose a topic to write about, (2) investigate the relevant literature, and (3) *summarize* and *critically evaluate* the research in an original paper. The literature search typically involves reviewing books and book chapters, review articles, primary source journal articles, and other sources. Increasingly, research on the Internet and the World Wide Web is available as well (but be careful of electronic sources because information published on the Net or Web has not typically undergone editorial review).

What a Term Paper in Psychology Should Contain

While all term papers have many basic similarities, term papers in psychology courses also often differ from those in many other disciplines in important ways. Although there is a great deal of variability in assignment and expectation among courses and instructors, most psychology term papers require that students do the following:

- **Choose a relatively specific topic, model, theory, or work of an important psychologist to write about.**
- **Complete a summary and a critical review, and suggest topics or areas where future research is needed.**

Many aspects of writing term papers in psychology are similar to those of critical evaluations of research articles, discussed earlier in this chapter. The main differences are that (1) a great deal more library research is usually required when preparing term papers, (2) the level of detailed description of individual research papers is less, and (3) because many sources are often cited, a great deal more organization and integration is needed.

When you write a term paper, you must:

- **Choose a topic.**
- **Develop a preliminary organization.**
- **Research the literature on that topic.**
- **(Re)organize your outline,** and finally,
- **Draft the paper itself.**

(You may have noticed that the first four of these points are included under Predrafting as part of the writing process in Chapter 3, while the fifth encompasses all aspects of the drafting process itself.)
Let's review each of these.

Choosing a Topic

Unless a topic is assigned, students usually find that putting some thought and effort into what topic they would like to investigate pays handsome dividends later.

A way to begin the process of topic selections is to apply the informal writing of your reading response log (see Chapter 2) as you review the **table of contents** and **index** of your textbook and the **topics identified** on your course syllabus. Topics listed in these sources are certainly relevant to the content of the course. Once you have identified three or four potential paper topics, spend a few hours reading and writing about some recent summaries and representative abstracts of relevant articles on each potential topic. In your writing, ask yourself which of the possible topics seems most interesting and which appears to be the best candidate for a critical review.

Before making a final determination of your topic, be sure to **discuss it with your instructor,** even if this step is not required. If you have taken notes in your reading response log, you will have something to show your instructor that can help him or her in giving advice. Your instructor may have suggestions for directions your paper may take or of sources you can use to find information on your topic.

Breadth of the Topic

Be sure that your topic is the proper breadth for the number of pages you plan to write. A topic like "parallels of language development in deaf and hearing children" (the one chosen by Jennifer Wilkinson for the paper we will present later in this chapter) is much more manageable than one like "psychology of the hearing impaired." You should make certain that you can adequately cover your topic in the time and space that you have available. Again, your instructor's advice can be invaluable.

Developing a Preliminary Organization

Your review of possible paper topics should allow you to develop a preliminary outline of the topics your paper will cover. Again, your log can be an invaluable tool in this process. *Example:* If your topic is "parallels of language development in deaf and hearing children," you may decide that you will start with a brief overview of language development in children and follow it with more specific descriptions of how deaf and hearing children show parallel aspects of language development and have similar milestones in language acquisition. You will probably also want to include sections, perhaps toward the end of your paper, that point out important differences between the languages of the two populations and suggests ideas for future research. **The preliminary organization may not represent the final structure of your paper, but it will guide the way you conduct your literature search.**

Just as in writing papers in other disciplines (and, to a substantial degree, in writing lab reports in psychology, discussed in Chapter 4), the best organization to follow is to start with (1) a broad introduction and review of general issues, then (2) progressively narrow the topic you are discussing. The first few paragraphs, which we will call the **first section** of your paper, should present the reader with an **overview** of your topic and **identify the goals** you have set. Before you begin discussing specific issues, you should clearly state the parameters under which you will be operating. (See Figure 5.1.)

- First section: Topic overview and identification of goals
- Middle section: Specific topics and issues
- Concluding paragraphs: Critical evaluation

FIGURE 5.1   Organization of a Term Paper

The **middle sections** of your paper usually address your **specific topics and issues.** Here is where you discuss the specific issues that you prefaced at the beginning of the paper. Organization should reflect these topics and issues and clearly point to relationships among them. A helpful procedure in writing this part of a term paper is to organize it by drafting a **topic sentence** for each paragraph. That is, the first draft begins with the potential topic sentence for each of the paragraphs that is likely to appear in the final draft. Supporting information, in the form of the remaining sentences of each paragraph, is initially withheld until the structure of the paper is drafted. Once you are satisfied that the draft topic sentences that you have written represent a structure that you would like the paper to adhere to, begin writing the rest of this portion of the paper—consisting of additional supporting information—in each paragraph. Of course, the final draft may reflect a somewhat different structure, but by organizing by topic (through initially drafting topic sentences) you can be sure that your organization will make sense to the reader.

In the **concluding paragraphs** or **section** of your paper, you often present a **critical evaluation of the research you have reported,** pointing out, for example, what conclusions were warranted and where more research is called for. Here is where you can be a research critic and evaluate the state of our knowledge of the topics and issues at hand.

Conducting the Literature Search

As we suggested in Chapter 3, by far the greatest amount of time preparing a term paper is spent searching for and summarizing research articles, reviews, book chapters, and other sources that pertain to the paper topic. The process may sometimes become disheartening if too many potential sources fail to yield usable information. But nearly every investigation will include some literature search dead ends as well as some pathways that end with new and important findings. But how do you know where to look?

Reading Recent Reviews

A good initial source of information is recent reviews related to your topic. These can often be found in chapters of recent professional books and book chapters, and recent issues of *Psychological Review* and *Annual Review of*

Psychology. You can use the references in these reviews to find important primary source articles (that is, articles that report the original research) on your topic. You need to be careful, of course, to ensure that your paper is not simply a "review of a review" and that it goes beyond simply summarizing what you find in one or two major articles.

Using Research Indexes and Databases

Your search for information should also include *Psychological Abstracts,* an American Psychological Association publication that includes brief summaries of virtually every article in psychology that has been published since the 1920s. It is updated monthly and is indexed by both author and research topic. The APA also publishes *PsycINFO* and *PsycLIT,* two computerized databases. Most university libraries subscribe to *PsycLIT* (Martin, 1996), a database that includes both recent journal articles and book chapters.

A different approach to finding appropriate sources is used in *Social Sciences Citation Index.* This publication identifies the references cited in journal articles. If an important and frequently cited article appeared in a journal several years ago, that article can be used as the source for more recent research. Each later edition of the index includes all the journal articles reviewed during the period that includes the critical article in the reference section. If you use this index, however, you need to remember that it does not include citations in books and book chapters or articles from journals that did not reference the article you are using as a source. Thus, the *Social Sciences Citation Index* should not be your only source of potential material.

Reading the Literature: Being Selective

Your search of abstracts and computer databases often yields huge numbers of potential sources, often far more than you can read carefully in the time that you have to prepare the paper. Thus, what strategies do you use in deciding what to pay attention to?

1. Read the abstracts. Depending on how you found your sources, abstracts may already be available. If not, you will have to find the articles and read the abstracts published there. Remember, an abstract is a brief and concise summary of a journal article or paper presentation that includes the purpose, method, results, and conclusions of the research described in the article (see Chapter 4). If the abstract indicates that the article is not important, you can then skip it. However, be sure to keep a record in your log of the articles you have *not* read in case your later findings make some of them appear relevant after all.

2. Read the article (or at least part of it). If your reading of an abstract makes it appear that an article may be important for your paper, you should read at least part of the article itself. A good strategy is to read carefully the **parts of the Introduction that develop the hypothesis** and the **parts of the Discussion that present the conclusions.** You will probably also want to attend to the **Procedure** described in the **Method** section, at least to get a general idea of what the investigator did. The **Introduction** and **Discussion** sections may include descriptions and conclusions from additional studies you may want to read. **Keep careful notes of important aspects of the study in your log.**

3. Make judicious use of photocopies. Many students find it valuable to make photocopies of important articles they find. This is a good, though sometimes expensive, idea. If you have your own copies of articles and book chapters, you can mark on them as you want. However, the time and expense spent feeding money into a photocopy machine will pay off *only* if the photocopied article turns out to be useful. A general recommendation is to be sure to at least skim an article for its relevance to your topic before making a photocopy of it.

4. Develop a spreadsheet. It is often helpful to develop a **spreadsheet** that includes, at a minimum, the reference, the purpose of the study (including the hypotheses, where appropriate), type of study design, results, and conclusions of each relevant study. A spreadsheet is a variant of a reading response log. Your spreadsheet should also include a space for relevant comments that distinguish studies from one another and for ideas you may want to develop in your paper. The spreadsheet will allow you to more easily compare and contrast the research you are reviewing as you write the paper.

A spreadsheet can serve as a better organized and more easily understood substitute for the "index card" method. The **index card method** is a time-tested procedure in which the content of each important literature source is summarized on its own index card. We believe that a spreadsheet is better because it (a) forces paper writers, if they want to complete all the columns on the spreadsheet, to pay attention to important aspects of the research which might have otherwise been overlooked; (b) allows writers to make direct comparisons across literature sources easily; and (c) permits easy organization and reorganization of the material. Thus, spreadsheets encourage paper writers to understand their sources in depth and to compare and contrast the content of multiple research articles.

Here is an example of information that might be included on a spreadsheet from one of the references in the example term paper at the end of this chapter. Please note that we haven't put it in spreadsheet format because there is not room on this page. However, the information is the same.

Reference: Masataka, N. (1992). Motherese in a signed language. *Infant Behavior and Development, 15,* 453–460.

Purpose: To see whether mothers use a form of motherese (slowing motions, exaggerating, repetition, etc.) when signing with their deaf infants.

Participants: 7 deaf Japanese mothers (Japanese sign language was their first language), each signing to her 8–11 month old infant and 1 deaf friend.

Method: Videotaped interaction. Measured average length of signs, repetition rate, angle subtended by hand, and angle subtended by elbow. Had 2 trained observers make judgments (high agreement in ratings).

Results: All 4 measures were significant: signs to infant slower, more repetitious, and showed greater hand and elbow angles.

Conclusions: (a) shows same pattern as motherese in speaking; (b) mother may try to adjust signs according to her perception of the attention and comprehension of child.

Notes: (a) Is motherese "natural" for signing? (b) Are deaf children's signing capacity related to earlier experience with motherese? (c) May want to have separate "motherese" section in final paper.

5. Keep accurate records of citations. By all means, keep an accurate record of the correct citation of each reference! Articles *must* be cited correctly in your Reference section. Countless hours have been wasted by students' having to "refind" articles in cases where accurate records of sources are missing. It also frequently occurs that sources initially deemed irrelevant turn out later to be important. So even if you initially think a source is not going to give you any pertinent information, it is wise to keep track of its reference.

(Re)organizing Your Outline

As you are reading your potential references, you will probably revise, or at least fine-tune, the organization of your paper. Your original structure was based on only a preliminary overview of your topic. As you delve further into your sources, you are likely to find some topics that should be expanded as well as some that seem less important than they did at first blush. You may even want to narrow your topic somewhat. It is not uncommon that students find a great deal more information on the topic they initially selected than they expected at the outset. **Of course, be sure that your instructor approves before you make any substantive change in the paper topic.**

Drafting the Paper

Now comes the product of your research endeavors and predraft writing! If you have developed a good organizational structure and if your library research has proven fruitful, drafting often proceeds quickly and easily. Sometimes drafting involves primarily reorganizing and expanding your notes, relating and summarizing your various subtopics, and developing critical analyses of your sources and proposed directions for future research.

A good strategy to use at this point is the **dummy draft** described in Chapter 3. This informal technique is a valuable stepping stone to a good rough draft. In addition, much of the same summary and evaluation discussed in the first half of this chapter is relevant to drafting term papers.

Some Drafting Points to Keep in Mind

As you write your paper, here are a few additional suggestions to remember.

1. Don't forget to evaluate. Good term papers are much more than a simple summary of research or theory. An evaluation component should be included as well. As you read each of your sources, you should take some time to think of its implications. **These thoughts should be recorded on a section of your spreadsheet.** The records you keep will often point to issues that you may want to develop in your paper. Let's look at some of the things you might find in your literature search that may kindle your curiosity.

You may find that the research that you review includes studies that draw conclusions that are at odds with one another. If you find this, it would certainly warrant your looking into reasons for the discrepancy. You may want to compare and contrast the methods, analyses, and other strategies the investigators used. This exercise may lead you to conclude that the differences resulted from the respective procedures that were used.

But you may then decide that one of the conclusions is more valid than the other (that is, because the procedure is more appropriate for answering the research question). Then you must explain and defend your choice. Of course, your explanation must come from well-reasoned comparisons of the studies in question, and you must present a convincing argument for your decision. **Presenting a personal opinion without providing rational bases for it does not help resolve different conclusions if they come from empirical research.**

Sometimes you may decide that different conclusions result from differences in methods or participants and are not really in conflict after all. If that is the case, be sure to discuss the differences in your paper and highlight what the investigators did that led to their respective conclusions.

Regardless of your conclusions, you should be sure to address the different outcomes that you uncover. A complete and well-written term paper should acknowledge inconsistencies in research results and attempt to explain their bases.

Sometimes you may feel that a whole line of research rests on questionable assumptions. *Example:* Alba and Hasher (1983) wrote an extensive critical review of the validity of understanding learning and memory research within the context of mental structures or *schemas.* They pointed out that a great deal of the research that supports schema theory is based on assessment of what participants did in unusual experimental tasks. For example, in some studies, people were asked to recognize whether a large number of sentences on topics they had just read about were repeated word for word or paraphrased from the original presentation. Alba and Hasher pointed out that this type of task is unusual outside a laboratory setting. It is rare that we learn information by rote memorization of related sentences. Thus, these results may be limited in their generalizability outside the laboratory setting.

Yet another way to evaluate a research paper is to examine its credibility for addressing the researcher's questions. You may want to identify potential fallacies in the way the research was conducted. Again, however, please remember that your opinion is only as good as the rationale behind it. Be sure to justify in a logical or rational way why you concluded what you did.

2. Organize your review by topic, not by the chronological order of the research you are citing. A topic-by-topic review informs your reader in an organized way of the main issues you are discussing. It allows for easy comprehension by the reader, and it presents an obvious basis for a critical analysis of the research.

A chronological review fails to recognize that research addresses different topics over time. If a chronological order is followed, later research may not clarify or follow from earlier studies. Even within subsections of your paper, where you are addressing specific topics, presenting your summary in a chronological order of citation dates may obscure some of the important findings of different studies.

3. Divide your paper into subsections and separate them with headings. Readers will have a much easier time understanding your paper if it is subdivided according to the topics you are discussing. A 15-page paper that does not identify topics by separate headings often appears rambling and unfocused. Readers have difficulty identifying when the topic under discussion is changing and what the important points are that you are trying to make.

The number of subsections you use depends on your paper topic and the paper's breadth. But if you find that more than four or five pages go by between appearances of section headings, your paper probably needs some editing. Readers must know what topic is currently under discussion.

Earlier in this chapter, we described a term paper as consisting of a **first section, middle sections,** and **concluding paragraphs,** and briefly identified what would normally be included in each of these. Usually these sections make for natural subdivisions, and each of these subdivisions can be identified by the relevant heading.

4. Use quotations sparingly. Every time you quote another author, you reduce the proportion of the paper that you are personally composing. **Quotations should be used only when they are necessary to illuminate and clarify the topic under discussion.** For example, if two investigators present definitions of a psychological concept that differ slightly from one another, and this difference may have affected their conclusions, quoting the two definitions will probably clarify the discussion in your paper. However, it is never correct to simply quote sentences or paragraphs from a paper in order to summarize that paper's content or to express your own conclusions. Instructors are not interested in whether the investigators whose works you are reviewing can write. They are interested in your summary and evaluation of the work. You will find that nearly all instructors frown on extensive use of quotations.

5. Avoid use of jargon. One of the authors of this book once had an article he had submitted for publication returned for rewrite because it included too much "jargonistic phraseology." In rereading the paper, he realized that nearly every technical term had been abbreviated and that some of the sentences looked more like collections of acronyms than well-formed sequences of meaningful words.

To avoid jargon in writing a paper, try to judge whether it will make sense to a reader who is not as well versed on the topic as you are. After all, you just spent countless hours reading, writing, and thinking about the topics in your paper, so a term or concept that has now become very familiar to you may still be obscure to someone who has not delved extensively into the topic. Even your course instructor may not be as familiar as you are with the material you are investigating. While technical terms abound in psychology, it is the writer's responsibility to be sure that these terms are understood.

Sample Term Paper

Now let us read an annotated term paper written for a class in child psychology by student Jennifer Wilkinson. Jennifer has incorporated the suggestions included in this chapter into her paper. As you read it, we think you'll find that it is very well organized and easy to follow.

Language Development 1

Abstract ──────────────────── A concise summary of
        Although much of the research on language   the paper. (See
development has focused on hearing children,   Chapter 4 for
more research is starting to be done to study   complete description
the process of language acquisition in deaf   of Abstract.)
children. Researchers have found that deaf
children go through stages of babbling (Petitto
& Marentette, 1991), private speech (Jamieson,
1995), and grammar construction (Crowson,
1994). Furthermore, the parents of deaf   Order of topics in
children facilitate the acquisition of language   Abstract follows that
by using manual "motherese" (Masataka, 1992)   of paper.
and varied and frequent signing (Spencer,
1993). This research shows that language
development in deaf children is similar to
language development in hearing children,
although large individual differences exist
among the deaf population. Suggestions for
future research are made.

Language Development 2

Parallels of Language Development in
Deaf and Hearing Children

Jennifer Wilkinson

    Much of the past research on language
development has focused on auditory language
learned by hearing children. Recently,   First section of paper
researchers such as Jamieson (1995) and   is broad: an overall
Masataka (1992) have begun to study whether   summary of language
language acquisition proceeds in the same   development.
manner for deaf children as for hearing
children. Results from studies of hearing
children learning different languages have

shown that the first stage in the acquisition
of language is babbling, which usually appears
between 7 and 10 months (Lane, Hoffmeister, &
Bahan, 1996). Next, between the ages of 12 and
18 months, children make one-word utterances,
and by 22 months, most children are at the two-
word utterance stage. Children begin to modify
words and learn rules for sentence construction
by 36 months (Lane et al., 1996).

Parents play an important role in the
language development of their children. One
unique manner in which parents, and many other
adults, talk to children is called "motherese."
Motherese is characterized by short sentences,
changes in voice fluctuation, slow tempo, and
repetition of words. The properties of
motherese are thought to enhance early language
acquisition by eliciting the infant's attention
and demonstrating important aspects of the
language (Masataka, 1992). Also, the richness
of the language environment the child is
exposed to, usually measured by the frequency
and type of word the child hears, is positively
correlated with the development of language
(Levine, 1981).

*A general description
of language
development in
hearing children.*

Children also take active control of
language learning. Through babbling, by which
an infant repeats consonant and vowel
combinations, the child gains experience in
language. Once the child reaches the level of
speaking word sequences in the native language,
he or she begins to acquire grammatical rules
for sentences (Berk, 1997). Although children
in this stage frequently make grammatical
mistakes, these mistakes are evidence that
children are learning and thinking about
grammatical rules (Crowson, 1994). Private
speech, or speech that is spoken aloud but not

Language Development 4

meant for the benefit of others, is another milestone in the language development of children. Private speech is a factor in cognitive development that helps link thought and language (Jamieson, 1995).

Language Development in Deaf Children ——————— *The first section continues: an overview of language development in deaf children.*

So far, language acquisition has only been discussed in terms of children who learn language by hearing those around them speak. However, there is a substantial subset of children who cannot do this because they are deaf. Most of the research in the past dealing with language development has focused on hearing children, and many of the ideas which come from that research have had an auditory basis. Recently, researchers have begun studying deaf children to see if their processes of acquiring language are similar to those of hearing children. Researchers have studied whether parents of deaf infants use a type of motherese in their communications with their infants and whether the signed language environment has an effect on the language development of children (Masataka, 1992; Spencer, 1993). Also, other researchers have focused on whether babbling occurs in deaf children and whether deaf children use a form of private speech (Petitto & Marentette, 1991; Cook & Harrison, 1995). In addition, some research has looked at the errors deaf children make in learning sign language and has compared them to errors made by hearing children learning spoken language (Crowson, 1994).

The middle sections: specific topics where development of deaf and hearing children is similar. Topic 1: "motherese."

Motherese. One experiment to determine whether deaf mothers use a form of manual motherese to communicate with their deaf babies was performed by Masataka (1992). Eight deaf mothers whose first learned language was

Language Development 5

Japanese Sign Language were each observed
interacting with her firstborn deaf infant and
also with an adult deaf friend who also signed
in Japanese Sign Language. These interactions
were videotaped and the signs were transcribed
by two independent observers who recorded the
duration of signs, the levels of exaggeration
of the signs, and the number of repeated signs.
Masataka found that the mothers repeated
significantly more signs when communicating
with their infants than when communicating with
their adult friends. Also, the duration of the
individual signs directed toward the infants
was longer than signs directed toward the
adults. Finally, the mean scores for the
maximum and average values of the angles for
each sign were significantly larger when the
signs were aimed at the infant.

These results led Masataka (1992) to
conclude that deaf mothers do use a manual form
of motherese when communicating with their deaf
infants. As in spoken motherese, there was more
repetition of symbols, a slower rate of
delivery, and exaggerated presentation.
Masataka suggested that manual motherese
elicits stronger responses from infants and
helps them to better acquire sign language.

Sign Language Development and Hearing
Parents. Hearing parents can also benefit their
deaf children by using sign language as a form
of communication. Spencer (1993) observed the
play between seven mothers and their deaf
infants. The families were all participants in
various intervention programs that were
designed to help deaf children acquire
language. A trained professional spent three-
to-five hours per week in the home teaching
parents sign language and providing other

*Topic 2: Relationship
between amount of
linguistic communica-
tion and language
development.*

Language Development 6

services for the parents and infant.
Researchers observed the mother and child
playing together and recorded the language
productions of the infants and the mothers. The
mothers also took part in three structured
interviews. Spencer reported that mothers who
signed often when their infants were 12 months
old continued to sign, often more frequently,
when their infants were 18 months old. The sign
production of infants at 18 months was
positively correlated with the number and
variety of signs that mothers produced six
months earlier. She also found that some of the
infants were capable of expressive language
during the same time frame as their hearing
counterparts, even though the number of signs
produced by the deaf infants' mothers did not
reach the number of words spoken by mothers of
hearing children.

Spencer (1993) concluded from these results
that infants' acquisition of sign language was
related to the quantity of signs the mother had
used. In general, an environment rich in
signing, even non-fluent signing, helped the
infants acquire language in a time frame equal
to that of hearing children.

"Sign Babbling" and Private Speech. Deaf
and hearing children also exhibit similarities
in the early stages of language acquisition.
Petitto and Marentette (1991) gathered
experimental and naturalistic data from two
deaf infants of deaf parents and three hearing
infants of hearing parents. The deaf infants
were in the process of acquiring American Sign
Language (ASL) as their first language, and the
hearing infants were not exposed to sign
language. All infants' manual activities were
recorded and examined for evidence of sign

*Topic 3: Private
speech.*

babbling. Petitto and Marentette found that
although deaf and hearing infants displayed
equal numbers of gestures, deaf infants
produced more sign babbling than did hearing
infants. The deaf infants engaged in manual
babbling by 10 months of age (the youngest age
tested), the same time frame in which their
hearing counterparts developed vocal babbling.
Furthermore, stages of sign babbling paralleled
stages of vocal babbling, and, as in vocal
babbling, frequently used phonetic units in
sign babbling were involved in the most
frequent first babbling units of deaf infants.

Because of these parallels between manual
babbling in deaf infants and vocal babbling in
hearing infants, Petitto and Marentette (1991)
concluded that language acquisition was
universal and not reliant on the development of
the vocal tract. Instead, they argued, because
babbling occurred at approximately the same
time in hearing and deaf infants, language
acquisition was based on a timetable of brain
maturation. This brain language capacity was
able to process different types of signals,
both manual and vocal, resulting in
similarities in language development between
deaf and hearing infants.

Another similarity between language
development of deaf and hearing children is the
occurrence of private signing in deaf children.
Private signing has the same characteristics
and serves the same function as private speech
does for hearing children (Cook & Harrison,
1995). Private speech is uttered aloud, but is
not produced for the benefit of communicating
with others. In the Cook and Harrison study,
teachers filled out one survey for the most
literacy-developed and the least literacy-

Language Development 8

developed preschool students and gave the
parents of these selected students surveys to
complete. The surveys included a section on
private signing that was answered only by
teachers and parents of students who used sign
language. Cook and Harrison found that a high
percentage of both the most advanced and least
advanced students used private sign in the
classroom and at home, although the advanced
students showed a greater incidence in some
learning situations. Deaf children signed to
themselves when they read privately as well as
when they played with toys and acted out
stories. Also, private sign was used to express
emotions and for self-regulation. Hearing
children use private speech for all these
activities.

In another study, Jamieson (1995) examined
the use of private speech among two groups of
deaf children. One group consisted of three
deaf children with hearing mothers, and one
consisted of three deaf children with deaf
mothers. All mother-child dyads that included
hearing mothers came from homes where English
was the primary language, while all dyads that
included deaf mothers used ASL as the primary
language in the home. Jamieson presented each
child with a task that was originally beyond
his or her ability level. The mother was asked
to teach the child how to complete the task,
and then the child performed the task alone.
Jamieson observed that children of deaf mothers
used private speech in a signed form. Deaf
children of hearing mothers also used private
speech, but at only 20 percent of the frequency
of those with deaf mothers.

Jamieson (1995) also concluded that
children of deaf mothers use a more mature form

Language Development 9

of private sign. Her study showed that their
signs were more task oriented and were used to
guide and monitor their performance. In
addition to the greatly reduced frequency of
private sign among deaf children of hearing
mothers, one-third of these signs were not task
related, involving instead word play and
repetition. Jamieson attributed this
discrepancy between groups to differences in
language exposure. Unlike children of hearing
mothers, those with deaf mothers had been
exposed to ASL from birth. Therefore, their
signed language environment was richer and more
conducive to development. A shared language
between parent and child seems to facilitate
the development and use of private sign.

    <u>Types of Errors</u>. Another important aspect
in the development of language is the type of
errors children make when acquiring language.
Crowson (1994) studied videotapes of six deaf
children from hearing families to determine
what types of errors they made in signing.
Errors were divided into four categories:
phonological, morphological (errors and
omissions), overgeneralizations, and other
types of errors. Crowson found that
phonological errors were the most common, with
handshape, movement, and orientation being the
most common. Although morphological errors and
overgeneralizations were also made, most of the
children had not yet reached the level
of signing where those errors would have
occurred.

    Crowson (1994) concluded that errors made
by deaf children were parallel to errors made
by hearing children at similar stages of
language acquisition. The phonological errors
in signing matched pronunciation errors made by

*Topic 4: Types of
errors.*

Language Development 10

hearing children. Handshape, movement, and orientation errors consisted of units from the sign language that the children were learning. Crowson also concluded that the overgeneralizations and morphological omissions matched semantic overgeneralization and morphological errors made by hearing children.

Thus, it can be concluded that deaf children tend to acquire language in approximately the same manner as hearing children. Just as parents of hearing children help their children develop language by using motherese and by providing a rich language environment, parents of deaf children help their children in the same manner (Berk, 1997). Deaf parents tend to use a manual form of motherese (Masataka, 1992), and parents who show a higher frequency of signing produce deaf children with better signing skills (Spencer, 1993). Deaf children exhibit sign babbling at the same time periods and with the same uses as hearing babies (Petitto & Marentette, 1991). In addition, deaf children use a form of private speech, termed private sign, that is similar to private speech in hearing children (Cook & Harrison, 1995; Jamieson, 1995).

Differences between Deaf and Hearing Children

Despite the parallels of language development between deaf and hearing children, there are also important differences. Deaf children as a whole have been shown to develop language skills at a slower rate than hearing children (Meadow, 1980). Within the deaf-children group, there is a large difference between language acquisition of deaf children with deaf parents and that of deaf children of hearing parents. Deaf children of deaf parents are more similar to hearing children of hearing

Note that topics concerning similarities between deaf and hearing children are presented consecutively. These make up the primary focus of the paper.

Now the main topic changes: the discussion concerns differences between deaf and hearing children.

Language Development 11

parents because the parents and child share a
common form of language (Lane et al., 1996).
Deaf children of hearing parents, on the other
hand, have a more difficult time learning
language because they typically will not
develop the same natural language as their
parents. Thus, there is little or no parent-
child linguistic communication (Lane et al.,
1996).

These differences become more apparent when
children reach school age. Deaf children of
deaf mothers have higher reading and writing
scores than their counterparts with hearing
mothers (Meadow, 1980). Although most deaf
children score in the normal range on IQ tests,
they perform below their potential in school.
These children, most of whom have hearing
parents, have not reached the level of language
comprehension and usage that allows them to
function well in academic settings (Meadow,
1980).

An elaboration of some of the differences.

Language also affects social and behavioral
aspects of deaf children. Deaf children of
hearing parents have less exposure to language,
delaying language development. This limits
their social interaction. They also have more
behavioral problems than deaf children of deaf
parents (Meadow, 1980). Levine (1981) suggests
that the shared language experienced by deaf
children of deaf parents fosters better
communication skills, producing fewer
interpersonal difficulties. Deaf children of
deaf parents are rated as more mature by their
teachers than deaf children of hearing parents
(Meadow, 1980).

One other difference between language
acquisition of deaf and hearing children
relates to individual differences. Probably due

Language Development 12

to the language environment that the child is raised in, there are greater individual differences in language development of deaf children. It is vitally important that deaf children be exposed to some type of manual communication. Deaf children need to be able to understand what is going on around them and to communicate their needs and feelings to others. Studies have shown that learning sign language does not inhibit learning oral language (Meadow, 1980), so parents should give their deaf children every opportunity to learn sign language. Also, to foster parent-child communication, parents should themselves learn sign language. Every child should be able to communicate with his or her own family.

Future Research

Future research into language development in deaf children should focus on obtaining larger sample sizes. Nearly all the studies reported in this paper used small sample sizes (usually six or seven children). Since only 1 in 1000 children under the age of three is deaf, the sample population is reduced to begin with (Schein, 1989). Small sample sizes reduce generalizability and lead to questions about the general applicability of the results. Studies like that of Cook and Harrison (1995) that have examined private sign and like that of Petitto and Marentette (1991) that have examined sign babbling have valid designs that could be replicated and extended by using larger numbers of participants.

Research into language development in deaf children has barely begun. It was not long ago that sign language was not considered to be a "natural language." Hockett (1960) suggested that one linguistic universal, that is, one

Concluding paragraphs: critical evaluation and suggestions for future directions for research.

Language Development 13

characteristic of all natural languages of the
world, was use of sound and voice for
communication. Recent research, pointing out
the similarities between language development
of deaf and hearing children, has clearly
identified sign language as parallel to spoken
language. However, much yet remains to be
discovered about the characteristics of sign
language development.

Language Development 14

References

Berk, L. E. (1997). Child development (4th
ed.). Needham Heights, MA: Allyn and Bacon.

Cook, J. H., & Harrison, M. (1995). Private
sign & literacy development in preschoolers
with hearing loss. Sign Language Studies, 88,
201-226.

Crowson, K. (1994). Errors made by deaf
children acquiring sign language. Early Child
Development and Care, 99, 63-78.

Hockett, C. F. (1960). The origin of
speech. Scientific American, 203, 89-96.

Jamieson, J. R. (1995). Visible thought:
Deaf children's use of signed & spoken private
speech. Sign Language Studies, 86, 63-80.

Lane, H., Hoffmeister, R., & Bahan, B.
(1996). A journey into the deaf-world. San
Diego: Dawn Sign Press.

Levine, E. S. (1981). The ecology of early
deafness: Guides to fashioning environments and
psychological assessment. New York: Columbia
University Press.

Masataka, N. (1992). Motherese in a signed
language. Infant Behavior and Development, 15,
453-460.

*References are
presented in APA
format: see Chapter 8.*

*References in the text
match exactly those in
the Reference section.*

*As in all parts of the
paper, references are
double spaced.*

Language Development   15

Meadow, K. P. (1980). <u>Deafness and child development.</u> Los Angeles: University of California Press.

Petitto, L. A., & Marentette, P. F. (1991). Babbling in the manual mode: Evidence for the ontogeny of language. <u>Science, 251,</u> 1493-1496.

Schein, J. D. (1989). <u>At home among strangers.</u> Washington, DC: Gallaudet University Press.

Spencer, P. E. (1993). The expressive communication of hearing mothers and deaf infants. <u>American Annals of the Deaf, 138,</u> 275-283.

Book

article

Analysis of the Sample Paper

As we have seen, Jennifer's paper started with an **overview** of her topic area and a **statement** of what her paper will concern. The middle sections examined **individual topics** in an easily readable and organized way, and the end of the paper discussed **possible problems** with the research that she reviewed and suggested **areas where additional research is needed.** This paper illustrates the importance of adequately discussing the procedures that investigators used and how their conclusions result from their empirical findings. Jennifer was able to show the parallels between language development of hearing and deaf children and make a strong case that sign language develops in a manner similar to that of spoken language. She also identified a few areas of difference in language development between the two populations and attempted to explain why they occur. By the end of her paper, readers had a clear grasp of language development by deaf children.

6

TAKING EXAMS

Psychology students are likely to encounter exams of different types in many of their courses. Some of these exams will require **no writing,** only marked responses to multiple-choice questions. Others may ask for **short written answers.** Still others may require **essays** of varying length and complexity. Some exams may combine these forms.

This chapter will deal with writing in each of these exam situations.

MULTIPLE-CHOICE EXAMS, TESTS, AND QUIZZES

Writing plays a role in your preparation for such exams, even though the exam itself requires no writing. The procedures in Chapter 2 for systematic **note taking** and regular **summarizing** use the power of writing to help you understand, remember, and apply course material. This regular thinking-through-writing pays off in better recall of information in timed testing situations.

Final Preparation Exercise

While the regular exercises described in Chapter 2 can make you feel more confident as you prepare for timed exams—thus reducing the last-minute anxiety commonly experienced by test takers—writing can also serve a purpose in that final preparation. In reviewing notes, summaries, and other materials (textbooks, lab manuals, etc.), use **further note taking** as a means to remember and think about important details. Test takers often read aloud or attempt to visualize terms or explanations they worry about forgetting. Instead, or in addition, take a few moments to write those items. In this way you use the power of writing to reinforce the knowledge you have acquired.

WRITING SHORT, TIMED RESPONSES: THE PRO SYSTEM

Students may be called on to write brief **definitions** of terms or brief **summaries** of procedures, among other short writing tasks on timed tests. In all timed writing situations, the most essential tasks for the test taker are:

1. Understanding the question's *content* and **purpose**
2. **Recalling** the pertinent information to meet that purpose
3. **Organizing** the information to make a clear presentation

This **purpose/recall/organization** sequence—**PRO** for short—is a writing process specifically helpful in the timed situation. It works as follows: Imagine the sample question

> In the space given, identify the seven standard parts of the lab report and define each.

1. Understand Purpose

Circle each key term needed to fulfill the task successfully *(space given, identify, seven, standard, lab report, define, each)*. Circling key terms helps you focus on all the important elements of the task.

Use a **question mark** to note any term that seems vague or difficult and that may cause you trouble in writing the response. For example, *standard* might mean "according to the APA manual," or it might mean "according to the format given for our first lab assignment." If the test-taking situation allows, you can use such markings to ask clarifying questions before attempting to write a response.

2. Recall All Pertinent Information

Again, if the testing situation allows you to use scrap paper—or the reverse sides of the exam pages—for making notes during the exam, use that space for some predraft writing (see Chapter 3, under Predrafting) to **recall** and **apply** everything pertinent to answering the test question.

If time allows (often it may not), a good predraft technique to use here is the **dummy draft** (see Chapter 3). Write without editing; your goal here is to get as much information onto the page as you can in a short amount of time; this isn't the place to worry about organization or neatness or good spelling. If you aren't sure of the accuracy or pertinence of something you write in this draft, mark it with a question mark, but don't stop now to think it through. When you've drafted the answer to the entire question, then go back to your question marks and work through your doubts—*if* time allows.

Sample Dummy Draft for Short-Answer Question

Title page—includes title, author, affiliation, running head

Abstract—written last; summarizes intro, methods, results, discussion; concise

Introduction—here you state the problem and give some background; often include a summary of the research and show how and why you've defined the scope of the experiment and the hypothesis

Method—detail how you proceeded, all the steps, and describe all materials and other conditions of the experiment (setting, etc.)

Results—summary of the data, but not *all* the raw data; just the key statistics, including levels of accuracy

Discussion—the significance of the results, especially how this experiment advances understanding of the problem; also, shortcomings of the research and type of further study needed

References—APA style; all the sources you used in the text, but only those; not a list of everything you consulted

Remember that time is of the essence. You may only have time to jot down an informal outline (notice that this dummy draft is little more than an outline, using phrases, not sentences); nevertheless, be sure to devote a portion of your time on the question to some sort of predrafting.

3. Organize *for a Clear Presentation*

After you've made a quick outline or quick **dummy draft,** go back to the question and double-check for clues about the **format** of the answer. In our sample, "In the space given, identify the seven major sections of the standard lab report and define each," the format is straightforward. Here's a revised response to the assigned task, based on the dummy draft just given:

The seven major parts of the standard lab report (as defined in lecture) are the *Title page, Abstract, Introduction, Method, Results, Discussion,* and *References*.

The *Title page* presents the title, author, location where the research was completed, and the running head.

The *Abstract* is written last and summarizes the Introduction, Method, Results, and Discussion sections very concisely.

The *Introduction* defines the problem, provides background (including a summary of the research literature on the topic), defines the scope of the experiment, and states the hypothesis.

The *Method* section describes in sequence all the procedures that were followed, lists all the materials used, and describes any other pertinent conditions. One goal of the section is to enable other researchers to conduct the experiment exactly as you did.

The *Results* section summarizes the data and reports all pertinent statistics, plus how they were calculated. Level of accuracy is crucial to report.

The *Discussion* analyzes the findings in order to state the significance of the experiment: Has the research hypothesis been adequately supported? To what extent? How do this experiment and the results advance our knowledge of the subject? What were the deficiencies of the experiment? What still needs to be done?

Finally, the *References* section lists in APA format all the sources you used in the report, but leaves out other works you merely consulted.

The best organization might not always be so easy to predict by rereading the question. However, even when the writer is in doubt, a few design principles always apply:

- You can safely give information **in the order in which it's asked.** Test readers usually must read quickly; if they don't find information where they expect to find it, they usually assume it's not present.
- Lay out the writing **so that the reader won't miss each section of the answer.** If the question asks for "seven main sections" and a definition of each, as in the sample, make sure your reader can easily see that you have included seven sections in your answer. For example, start a new paragraph with each section *or* leave white space after each.
- Even if the question offers no obvious format, *don't* put down information in the order in which you think of it; always arrange it in the order **in which a reader can most easily follow it.** Because writers usually think of ideas and details somewhat randomly and idiosyncratically, it's *essential* to take two steps: first, to recall, *then* to organize material. (See the next section, on "Writing Timed Essays," for a fuller discussion of options in organizing your answers.)

WRITING TIMED ESSAYS

Written examinations include **timed** and **untimed** (or "take-home") varieties. **Untimed** exams are similar to other types of paper assignments;

writing them follows the writing process model described in Chapter 3. This chapter will not address take-home exams separately.

Writing **timed essay exams** also follows the PRO system:

1. Understand the **purpose** of the question or topic
2. **Recall** all pertinent information
3. **Organize** the information so the reader can follow it easily

Step 1: Understand Purpose
(first fraction—1–3 min.—of allotted time)

In their haste to start writing, many exam takers stumble at the first step: **understanding the question or topic through close, careful reading.** Some fail to address all parts of a question; others, not reading closely, assume a question that's not being asked. Whatever the failing, even strong essays by well-prepared students lose credit for "not addressing the question."

Method: Read the exam question with pen in hand. **Circle** each key word as you read. Here's a sample:

Describe Craik and Lockhart's (1972) levels of processing model of memory. How is a memory trace formed, according to this model? Why is a distinction between maintenance and elaborative rehearsal important? (?)

Note the circled words. The writer has made the effort to identify every element that must be considered in composing an effective essay.

Note that besides *circling* words, the writer has also used the **question mark** to identify key terms that seem vague. *If the rules of the exam allow, ask the exam giver to clarify terms that you have marked in this way.*

Pay special attention to action verbs. Toward understanding the **purpose** of the question, the most important words in any assignment are often the **action verbs.** In the sample question, the one action verb is *describe.* However, the circled noun *distinction* implies the verb *distinguish,* while the circled adverb *how* implies the action verbs *describe* or *show,* and the circled words *why . . . important* imply the action verbs *explain* or *evaluate* or *prove.* Other common action verbs that appear in assignments include *analyze, categorize* (or *classify*), *compare* (or *compare and contrast*), *defend, define, discuss, list, recommend, reflect on, show* (or *demonstrate*), and *support* (or *substantiate*), among many others. Though you'll want to clarify these terms with the exam giver if they don't seem clear in the question, they mean roughly the following:

Analyze—break a problem into appropriate parts toward reaching an overall judgment or solution.

Categorize (or **classify**)—put information into appropriate classes or categories, which you define.

Compare (or **compare and contrast**)—state the similarities *and* differences between two or more phenomena; often you are expected to take a position in favor of one of the phenomena being compared.

Defend—provide evidence (usually empirical) for the conclusion you have drawn; see **prove.**

Define—in academic contexts, this does *not* mean looking up a term in Webster's Dictionary, though specialty dictionaries or encyclopedias in a discipline may be used as sources of definitions. **Defining** usually requires that you not only report **what** the term means but also **why** it means that; a good definition usually shows how a term can mean different things in different contexts.

Demonstrate—see **show.**

Describe—report the stages of a process in detail or the physical features of an object, place, or person; precision and substantial detail are usually required.

Discuss—one of the most common key words in assignments and one of the trickiest to define, because testmakers use it to mean a range of actions; it can mean *analyze, compare, describe,* or most of the other terms in this list. Often it means that you should (1) **evaluate** the significance of research results and apply them to other contexts, or (2) **identify** the major differing positions on a controversial topic and eventually arrive at a judgment based on a careful comparison. Often, **discuss** is followed by a clarification of the specific points that should be addressed; if not, **ask the exam giver to clarify this term!**

Distinguish—see **compare and contrast. Distinguish** usually emphasizes the contrast.

Evaluate—give a judgment on the value of, often in comparison with other examples or items; this judgment is not a simple "good" or "bad," but the result of reasoned analysis of pertinent factors—not only that an item *is* valuable, but also **how** and **why.**

Explain—give reasons or causes for a phenomenon; often paired with **describe.**

Identify—somewhat vague, it can be as formal as *define* or as informal as *list.*

List—simply, to place in an order that is asked for in the question (e.g., "from most to least important"); often paired with **define** or **explain.**

Prove—similar to **show** and **demonstrate;** often implied by **discuss;** in exam situations, it often means to state a hypothesis or take a position, and then give reasons or evidence to justify that hypothesis or position; in academic writing, **proof** often does not imply absolute or exclusive truth, but a reasonable judgment based on a careful, respectful weighing of items of evidence or different views.

Recommend—to state a preference among possible phenomena or courses of action; it usually implies that you give reasons and provide evidence to justify the recommendation.

Reflect on—similar to **discuss;** equally vague. Ask for clarification, if at all possible; in some cases, **reflect on** means to consider, in writing, how a phenomenon might be significant or how it might be applied to other situations than the one in which it commonly occurs.

Show (or **demonstrate**)—depending on context, means **prove, describe,** or **explain.** Read the question closely and ask for clarification, if necessary and possible.

Support (or **substantiate**)—similar to **explain;** often paired with **prove** or **take a position;** means to give reasons or evidence to justify a position. (See **prove,** especially the definition of **proof.**)

Step 2: Recall All Pertinent Information (roughly one-third of remaining time)

Again, because they are hurrying, many exam takers try to craft a "final" essay in response to a question without having gathered the information they need to write well. The PRO method includes a second step in which the writer calls up all the information pertinent to a strong answer before crafting the essay itself. This step saves time because it allows writers to concentrate on collecting information rather than also having to worry about organization, tone, correct grammar, and other final draft elements.

Because time is of the essence and because most exam situations don't allow writers to consult source material, we will describe two writing methods to promote quick recall from memory in timed essay contexts:

a. Outline Listing

After having carefully read and marked the question, create a quick outline of the kinds of information you'll need to answer the question. For instance, a person answering the sample question might write:

Describe the model

Describe how memory trace formed

Explain diff. between maintenance and elaborative and why diff. important

Then, in each category of the outline, brainstorm a list of the information you need for a strong answer. *Remember*, **brainstorming** means to write quickly without censoring what you write; your goal here is to get as much information onto the page in as short a time as possible. Here's a sample:

Describe the model

- *Continuous levels, not discrete stages*
- *Shallow vs. deep processing*
- *Many cycles, each going deeper*
- *Each cycle leaves a memory trace*

Describe how memory trace formed

- *Deeper processing, more complex traces*
- *More complex traces, better memory*

Explain diff. between maintenance and elaborative and why diff. important

- *Maintenance rehearsal = repet. at some level; elab. rehearsal = deeper processing*

b. Mind Mapping (aka clustering)

This well-known method allows you to locate information at various spaces on the page, rather than moving strictly top to bottom. The mind map begins with the writer placing the focal idea of the essay in the *center* of the page, then placing subcategories and further details—as the writer thinks of them—around the central idea:

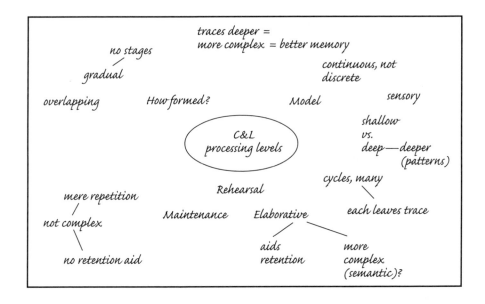

As you add information, you will become aware of connections among details and thus will draw lines between terms to show the connections:

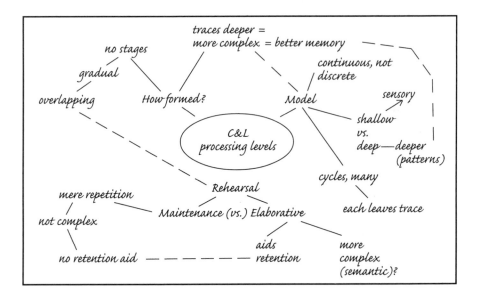

With these "clusters" of ideas displayed on the map, it is easy to turn them into an outline of principal topics:

Features of the model
How the memory trace is formed
Diff. between maintenance and elaborative and why diff. important

There is no need to "fill in" the outline, since all the subtopics are already displayed on the map.

Step 3: Drafting the Information in an Organized Format (remainder of allotted time)

The first and second steps of the PRO method should normally comprise about a third of the time you set aside to devote to the exam question. The final two-thirds of the time should be given to **drafting** the essay itself, with a small portion of that two-thirds left for **editing** and **proofreading.**

Caution: If you have not planned your time adequately, as sometimes happens, you may wind up with too little time to do an adequate job on Step 3 of the process. If this occurs, **it's better for you to write as your draft a poorly organized version of your Recall (Step 2) information than to leave the essay space blank.** While carefully following the steps will usually result in a strong essay, a disorganized answer may at least garner some credit.

Step 3 of the PRO method is very similar to the **Drafting** section of Chapter 3, and it would be useful to review that section when you are preparing to take essay exams. The great difference between the process described there and the process for exam taking is that the exam situation usually allows no opportunity for seeking **feedback,** hence no meaningful opportunity for **revision.**

You must cultivate a strong sense of the demands of your **audience**— usually the professor—before you take the exam, because there will be little or no chance to refine this sense by asking questions during the writing period. For example, does the professor look for general concepts? For specific references? Indeed, since most exams are taken well into and at the end of the semester course, one skill that is being tested is your understanding of what the professor expects.

Although the exam context doesn't allow you to fine-tune the essay for the professor, you can be sure of two essentials:

1. The essay should address **all** parts of the question.
2. It must be clearly organized.

We have addressed the first essential in Steps 1 and 2 of the PRO method. **Clear organization** is the province of Step 3.

Suggestions for Clear Organization

- **Well-organized exam essays usually adhere closely to the order suggested by the question.** That's one reason why close reading and marking of questions (Step 1) are so important. In a different circumstance, you may want to construct and order the essay differently; for the purposes of the timed writing situation, however, it's safest to put information where the reader expects to find it.
- **Well-organized exam essays use paragraphs, white space, and other format features to show the structure clearly.** If you have carefully followed the Recall portion of the PRO method, then arranging information in a clear layout should not consume much time. Not only will it provide easier reading for the exam grader, but it will show that person that you have carefully considered your answer and understand how parts of the information relate logically.

Sample Exam Essay (by student Angela Bruflat)

Describe Craik and Lockhart's (1972) levels of processing model of memory. How is a memory trace formed, according to this model? Why is a distinction between maintenance and elaborative rehearsal important?

Craik and Lockhart's levels of processing model views memory as continuous rather than operating in a series of discrete stages. According to this model, information is first processed at a shallow level (such as sensory memory), then, progressively, to a deeper level (such as pattern recognition), then to even deeper (for example, semantic) levels. The process of memory occurs in cycles, with each cycle building on previous ones as processing becomes deeper. These cycles are not like stages because stages imply that each level would involve qualitatively different types of processing. The levels of processing model asserts that processing levels overlap and that the shift to qualitatively different types of processing is gradual.

This continuum of processing leaves a residue of memory traces. Each processing cycle results in a trace. These traces build on each other and become more complex as processing reaches deeper levels. A more complex trace implies better memory access, so the deeper the processing the more likely a memory trace is to be remembered.

The distinction between maintenance and elaborative rehearsal is important because, according to the levels of processing model, maintenance rehearsal should not contribute to long-term retention because it is just a repetition at a shallow level of processing. Therefore, there is no development of a more complex trace. However, elaborative rehearsal consists of deeper processing and usually assigns meaning to the information (that is, usually involves processing to the semantic level). Since deeper levels of processing leave behind more complex memory traces, subsequent memory for that information is enhanced.

Notice how Angela has used the **data** and **patterns** from **Step 2** (Recall) to craft the essay. The writer has used paragraph breaks to show the professor at a glance that each of the three elements of the question has been answered.

Notice also that in drafting Angela has **gone beyond the details written in the outline** and has given special emphasis to the contrast between shallow and deeper processing in each paragraph. This difference between outline (or mind map) and draft illustrates that the outline, or mind map, should not be used to restrict further thinking in the draft itself.

EDITING AND PROOFREADING

Most exam graders, realizing the pressure of time in exam situations, have a higher tolerance for minor errors in exams than they do in reports and other documents. Nevertheless, a few minutes reserved for proofreading can help you identify not-so-minor errors and make a stronger impression on the grader.

Several categories to observe:

- **Accurate use of technical terms** (e.g., the limits of the model being discussed, the concepts the model predicts; procedures of the studies being presented to support your answer)
- **Accurate use of statistics** (Have statistics been cited accurately? Are numbers and symbols correct in formulae and equations?)
- **Accurate references to authorities** (e.g., researchers) and institutions (e.g., agencies, boards)
- **Clear sentence structure** (e.g., have any words been inadvertently omitted? Are **conjunctions,** such as *however, although,* and *nevertheless,* used correctly, so that the reader can follow your flow of thought? Are sentences long enough to convey your sophisticated ideas, but not so long as to confuse the reader?)
- **Correct spelling** (of relatively low priority in timed exams, so infrequent spelling errors should not be a source of anxiety for test takers).

A FINAL WORD TO THE WISE: ANSWER *ALL* QUESTIONS

Finally, the only way to ensure that you receive *no* credit for an essay answer is to leave it blank. Unless your instructor is imposing a penalty for answers that are "way off the wall," be sure to make an attempt to answer each required question. Many faculty will give a little bit of credit for any part of the answer that is close to being correct. Most veterans of the essay question wars can recall at least once when they "got lucky" on an answer.

7

ORAL PRESENTATIONS

Psychology students and graduates of psychology programs, just like nearly all other successful individuals, need strong, versatile speaking skills. Whether students go on to graduate school and prepare for careers as practicing professionals, researchers, or teachers, or use their degrees for entry into human resource positions, paraprofessional fields, or a host of other careers, the ability to make effective oral presentations to the public will be an important job skill. In addition, more and more courses in all college curricula require oral presentations. In upper-level psychology courses, students are often called on to give talks in special seminar classes or as part of a traditional curriculum. Thus, oral presentation skills can sometimes be as important as written presentation skills in both the classroom and the world of work.

This writing guide includes a chapter on oral presentation because:

1. Writing is an invaluable tool of **preparation** for public speaking.
2. Effective oral presentation often demands **written materials,** clearly and attractively designed, as part of the presentation.

This chapter will also briefly review some **time-tested tips** for effective speaking in public.

WRITTEN PREPARATION FOR THE TALK

For thousands of years, writing has been recognized as essential preparation for good speakers. The Roman rhetorician Quintilian regarded writing and speaking as inseparable. He says that writing improves the accuracy of our speaking, just as practice in speaking improves our ability to write.

While technology has changed communication in many ways over the ensuing centuries, the necessity for professionals in any field to put across their ideas orally has not diminished. Indeed, in the age of television and the multimedia Internet, those abilities—along with writing skill—will be perhaps more stringently tested than ever before.

Writing to prepare for talk usually includes:

1. Detailed, focused **note-taking** and **other predraft exercises**
2. Careful **outlining**
3. Either formal or informal **scripting** of the talk

Note: We do *not* recommend that speakers work from a prepared text as they speak. Later in the chapter we describe how to script a talk and prepare for the speech so that you can deliver a speech well without having to read it.

Note Taking and Other Predraft Exercises

See Chapter 2, under Writing and Memory: Taking Good Notes, for note taking techniques. Also see Chapter 2 for detailed descriptions of other tools for data collection, such as **annotating** your reading and keeping a **research log** or **spreadsheet**. See Chapter 3, under "Prewriting" and Data Collection, for description of other useful predraft techniques, such as the **dummy draft.**

If experienced writers typically devote 80 percent or more of their time on a project to predraft work, it's all the more important for speakers to invest this proportion of time. Speaking puts most of us under intense pressure to perform, and preparing thoroughly, so that we are confident of our materials, helps to relieve anxiety.

Write to Anticipate Audience Questions

Certainly you need to think about questions that readers are likely to raise in response to ideas that you write; such anticipation is a basic part of **audience awareness,** which we discuss from time to time throughout the book. But anticipating questions is especially important for the speaker, since an audience will demand an immediate response. Therefore:

- As you (1) collect data for a speech, as you (2) prepare a dummy draft or other predraft tool, and then as you (3) outline your talk, **keep a running list** of points that your audience is likely to find surprising or controversial—and that you may be asked to clarify or defend.

• Use this list to research and record information you might use to answer such questions. Even if you decide not to include this extra information in the talk itself, you will have done the search work necessary to back up controversial points—and you will be better prepared for audience questions.

For example, in preparing for a talk on public perceptions of group homes for the mentally ill (the sample topic explored later in this chapter), you might brainstorm the following questions as likely to be of concern to audience members:

"Aren't the mentally ill dangerous to children and others in a neighborhood?"

"What precautions are mental health officials required to take to ensure neighborhood safety?"

"Doesn't the presence of a group home reduce property values in a neighborhood?"

"What goals are meant to be achieved in placing group homes in residential neighborhoods? What proof is there that group homes meet these goals?"

As noted, questions like these might help you design your talk, but even if you do not choose to address them all in the talk itself, research you do in response will help you prepare for audience questions.

Careful Outlining

As you prepare to give your talk, one of your most important activities will be to arrange an **outline,** or a structure for your presentation. People are less adept at remembering what they hear than at remembering what they read—probably because they can't go back and review what they hear in an oral presentation. Therefore, it is critical that you organize your talk in a way that gives it the best chance to be memorable.

Most speakers outline their presentations simply as—outlines! They list their main points sequentially and indent subordinate points for each main point. This outlining method may work very well—after all, it is a tried-and-true procedure. However, it doesn't promote a presentation that will stand out in the minds of your audience. Listeners get only one chance to hear what it is that you have to say, so you must strive to be as dynamic and commanding (that is, as *memorable*) as possible. We recommend two different outline methods: **Telling Stories** and **"Q-and-A."**

Telling Stories

Everyone loves a well-told story. Stories give listeners a familiar framework on which to attach—and keep together—the flow of ideas. A well-told story is rich in mental imagery and allows the listener to become a participant in the unfolding plot. Sometimes a story can even be told with the emphasis on the second person. The word *you* liberally sprinkled throughout a presentation helps the listener personalize the talk's content. Psychologists have long known that if people apply traits or events to themselves, their memory is greatly enhanced. This phenomenon, called the **self-reference effect** (Rogers, Kuiper, & Kirker, 1977), has been investigated extensively since the late 1970s.

"How," you might ask, "can I make a story out of the presentation I have to make?"

Possibilities are everywhere. For example, the report of an experiment always contains the **method** that was used: "To select material for the experiment to see how people judged emotional expression, we had to find pictures of people showing different emotions. But we also needed to ensure that the people depicted were equally attractive to our subjects. Thus, we cut out 450 pictures from magazines and periodicals and had two students independently rate the attractiveness of the people in the pictures. Our criteria for selecting the 450 pictures were . . ." and so on. A well-prepared oral report should contain enough detail so that listeners who are unfamiliar with the topic can understand why the research was done, how it was accomplished, and what the conclusions were.

Outlining a talk **as a story** can mean taking advantage of story opportunities in any subject. For example, suppose a human resource specialist is discussing retirement plan options. She might tell stories about hypothetical workers and their long-term goals:

> Maria is a 23-year old customer service representative who is married and expecting her first child. Maria and her husband's combined income is $63,000. However, neither of them has started a retirement plan. . . .

Using a story makes the problem real to the listener. It ensures greater attention and understanding than boldly stating the point: "Even though they are just starting their families, twenty-three-year olds should be planning for retirement."

In a broader sense, however, outlining as a story means **interweaving a narrative through the entire oral report.** Note the difference between these two examples:

Sample 1 (not using a story frame)

> This report is about the depiction of mental illness in the mass media. A great deal of research has recently focused on how magazines, television, and

movies have misrepresented individuals suffering from various forms of mental disorders. Yet the media continue to greatly overstate risks of violence and unpredictable behaviors associated with mental illness. This report will summarize decades of research on this issue and describe the work of several people and organizations that are trying to educate the public about mental illness.

Sample 2 (using a story frame)

Suppose that you find, when you return home later today, that your neighbor's house, which has been up for sale for several weeks now, has been sold to an organization that plans on converting it into a group home for people suffering from mental illness. What would be your response? If you took your cues from the mass media, you would probably be concerned, for decades of research have found that magazines, television, and movies dramatically overemphasize risks of violence and unpredictable behaviors associated with mental illness. Later this evening, you turn on your television and watch a movie about an escaped mental patient who stalks and. . . .

The first sample presents a straightforward outline for a talk: a documented summary of research into unrealistic presentations of people with mental illness by the media, followed by a summary of recent efforts to change the stigma associated with mental illness. This outline is standard in written summaries of research. This format is used because readers expect certain types of information to appear in specific locations in written reports. It allows readers to skim such reports because they know where to look for certain kinds of information. They also know where to return to if they later want to engage in closer reading of some aspect of the report.

However, for an *oral presentation,* the story outline is usually better suited to ensuring that the listener will pay closer attention and won't miss many of the important points, because it involves the listener in the presenter's quest. Please note also that sample 2 used the second person *you;* the audience was encouraged to put themselves into the story itself. Notice that the "story" may actually unfold very much as the standard report does: the presenter will still probably first describe studies of media depictions of mental illness and then go on to describe what some psychologists and mental health organizations are doing to educate public perceptions.

What to Leave Out of the Story. Regardless of the presentation format used, listeners can't be expected to hold onto nearly as much information as a written report would contain. Therefore, the speaker will *leave out* of the talk many of the details (e.g., descriptions of the methods used in the studies being reviewed). Instead, the speaker will rely on **summaries** of research and findings and may back up the talk with **written material** (e.g., a handout summary) that contains more information. As with any good story, this one will be remembered better if it doesn't get bogged down in the mud of detail.

A caveat: Samples 1 and 2 and the one to follow in the next section should not be taken to imply that we encourage speakers to make their presentation from prepared text. These sections of the chapter have to do with outlining and preparing oral presentations. Later, we address the issue of speaking from an outline versus reading a prepared paper and come down firmly on the side of *not* reading. The examples are meant to illustrate different presentation formats. You can use any of these formats whether you are speaking from notes or reading an address.

Q-and-A

Question-and-answer structure is becoming ever more popular in professional writing and speaking. Like the story format, it relies on an age-old form, the **dialogue,** our everyday mode of conversation. Indeed, TV and radio talk shows and interviews have so institutionalized Q-and-A that it has in many contexts begun to replace the lecture (or sermon or political speech) as the standard oral mode of delivering information and opinion.

Of course, a talk organized around Q-and-A merely creates the illusion of dialogue, but it can be an effective ploy. Throwing out questions to your audience—especially if you include a "pregnant pause" before answering—can challenge your listener. It raises dramatic tension, and tension means attention.

Here is an excerpt from the talk on media depiction of mental illness as Q-and-A:

> Would you want someone suffering from mental illness to live next door to you?
>
> Not if you relied on the mass media (magazines, TV, movies, etc.) to understand what these people are like.
>
> But what is wrong with mass media depictions?
>
> Their illustrations are far more violent and show behaviors that are far less predictable than are really the case.

The key to using Q-and-A effectively as you are outlining your presentation is to **organize the questions in a logical way.** Start by brainstorming pertinent questions as they come to you—don't worry about order—then rearrange the questions in a way that a curious listener might logically ask them. Usually, doing this will lead you to add more questions to your outline and, maybe, deleting a few. As your outline develops, you may find that you need to rearrange the questions once again; and so forth.

Three more advantages of Q-and-A are:

1. Questions give you, the speaker, an excellent way to keep in mind all you have to say.
2. Questions make effective visuals on a screen or handout.
3. Questions give your listeners a clear framework for organizing and re-membering your talk.

Scripting: Speaking from an Outline versus Reading Your Talk

Speaking from an Outline

Novice speakers almost always seem to want to read their talks from a pre-pared script. But few of us have the training or skill to make a completely scripted text come across to an audience as sincerely spoken, not to mention interesting. Too many fully crafted talks wind up being read to an audi-ence—usually a deadly tedious experience—by a speaker who couldn't bear to leave out a word but didn't have the time or the skill—or perhaps the confidence—to deliver it without reading.

We strongly encourage that you avoid reading a prepared script and, instead, use a detailed outline to cue the points you are trying to make. In this case, "scripting" a talk means **drafting** and **revising** sufficiently so you feel you have **discovered** and **organized** everything you want to talk about. But you will leave much of the actual wording unscripted—to allow your-self to fill in the gaps spontaneously as you are speaking. This will allow you to make eye contact with the audience and make the speech seem spontaneous.

Here is an excerpt from the opening of the talk on media depiction of mental illness (note that the Tell a Story format has been used):

> Neighbor's house for sale; sold to organization for group home
> How do you feel?
> > Shaped by mass media: magazines, TV, movies
> > Overemphasize violence, unpredictable behaviors

Reading Your Talk

There are a few people—those who are really comfortable speaking in pub-lic, can maintain eye contact while reading, and can read at a reasonable rate while using appropriate voice inflection—who can be effective when reading from a prepared text. If you choose to read and feel that you can effectively make your oral presentation this way, **scripting** means preparing the verbatim presentation you will make. A few tips are in order for scripting a text to be read aloud:

- First, **remember that the talking script is *not* a text available to the audience**. Experienced readers can comprehend written text much faster than text that they hear. Thus, it is critical that reading speed be slow enough that the audience can follow the talk. It is also important that the reader differentiate by voice inflection and appropriate pauses the important points and the supporting material of the presentation.
- Second, **the use of such formats as Telling a Story and Q-and-A can help ensure that your audience will listen attentively and remember your ideas.**
- Third (and this is important), **practice your presentation before a practice audience** unfamiliar with what you are going to discuss. Constructive feedback during a practice session can inform you of potential problem areas, both in content and delivery. (See the "practice, practice, practice" tip later in this chapter.)

WRITTEN VISUAL AIDS

Although political speeches and religious sermons are still usually given without visual props, most professionals make their words more effective through graphics. These may run to the elaborate: videotapes, multilayered/multicolor graphs, Web pages on supersize projectors, and the like. Nevertheless, even simple uses of writing can add clarity and punch to a talk. For more complex uses of graphics, we've included a select list of sources at the end of this section.

If you want to keep it simple but still have impact, we suggest the following.

Your Simplified Outline

Don't include every subheading from your outline, but do provide your major topics (or questions, if you use Q-and-A) and some key terms you want your listeners to be sure to remember. A chalkboard, a poster, a flip chart, a transparency on an overhead projector, a one-page handout: any of these is suitable for a simple list. If possible, keep the visual outline to one page or screen that will remain before the audience throughout your talk and to which you can point as you move from idea to idea.

> Would you want someone with mental illness moving in next door to you?
>
> How do the media depict mental illness?
>
> What is wrong with the media depiction?
>
> How have some communities responded?
>
> What can you do?

A **more detailed outline** may work well as a handout to accompany the talk. As long as your remarks follow the outline, listeners can use the handout for note taking.

Idea or Flowchart

Use the two-dimensional space of the board, page, or screen to show relationships:

> *Responding to Media Depictions of Mental Illness*
>
> Media tendency to stress the violent and strange → Distorted depictions of mental illness → Community fears of the mentally ill → "Counter" campaigns by mental health organizations

Creating the Visual as You Talk

A dynamic way to use visuals is to build the outline or flowchart as you talk. As you work from your own outline, fill it in for your audience visually as you come to each new topic or question. You can do this by writing on the chalkboard, flip chart, or overhead transparency so that by the end of your talk the audience has a complete outline.

(Those adept at using overhead transparencies sometimes create a stack of these beforehand, with each new transparency adding another line or two to the outline. The speaker builds the stack, sheet by sheet, as the talk progresses. Further, those adept at using presentation software can use the screen to display one line of the outline at a time, keeping the audience guessing as the talk proceeds.)

Using Presentation Software

If you have the tools and if you're sure the technology will work, then you can be a bit more fancy and use presentation software. We have described the low-tech alternatives to this point because we have found them to be effective, reliable, and eminently portable to any location. But if you're sure there will be no technical glitches (though we've never known 100 percent certainty to be possible, even on our home turf), then why not add the extra pizzazz that presentation software gives?

These programs are becoming ever easier to learn, because (1) they tend to work reasonably like a word processor, and (2) what you see on the screen as you are composing is what you'll see on your paper or transparency as well as on the screen when you are presenting. Not only can you bring color, different fonts and type sizes, and interesting backgrounds to your visuals, but you can also experiment with art designs and video effects. Moreover, you can easily incorporate charts and graphs, if appropriate.

The Algorithm of Technology and Presentations

Keep in mind this rule of thumb as you are experimenting with technology for your presentation—the more complex the technology and the fancier the visual display, the more time you will have to invest in practicing with the technology to make sure that it works. If you are presenting at a location, such as a conference, with which you are not familiar, you will need to check and double-check—before you travel—with whomever is supervising the space to make sure that the facilities on location match your technical needs. When you are on site and before your presentation, be sure to try out the technology before your presentation—well before, if possible.

If you have any doubts about the reliability of the equipment on site, be sure to have a **low-technology backup.** For example, if you're not sure about projection capability, bring handouts or a poster-size flip chart. **Don't get caught with no visual capability.**

Additional Information in Handouts

If you have more information available to your audience in written form, you can without anxiety leave out many details from your talk that might intrude on their ability to remember your main points. Tell your audience about these additional materials wherever appropriate in the talk; however, we advise you *not* to distribute any of these materials *during* the talk because they will distract the audience.

TIPS FOR EFFECTIVE SPEAKING

The following will not substitute for a fuller guide (see the list of sources at the end of the chapter), but they can serve as a partial checklist as you prepare and practice.

1. Prepare, with writing as a help. Using the tactics described up to this point is the best way to ensure a good talk.

2. Practice, practice, practice. After you feel that your talk is in nearly final form, it is important to try it out, both in private and before a practice audience. As you practice in private, be sure to speak aloud and at the rate you expect to be delivering the presentation. Doing this will allow you to gauge the approximate time that your talk will consume and to become aware of problem areas in your presentation. During your first two or three run-throughs, have a pencil handy to indicate parts of the talk that you think may need some additional work or on which you may want to make some changes. After practicing in private, the next step is to ask some friends, fellow students, co-workers, or family members to listen and give you additional feedback. If possible, this practice audience should be similar, in education level and familiarity with the topic, to the audience that will finally hear your talk. Ask members of the practice audience to have paper and pencil handy and to jot down things that are not clear as the talk is given. Having them allow you to make your entire presentation without interruption will probably be more helpful than making you respond to questions and criticisms during the talk itself. Be sure that presentations before practice audiences are scheduled sufficiently early to allow for revision.

3. Speak distinctly, and more slowly than you would in normal conversation. Out of nervousness, inexperienced speakers often hurry their talks and fail to e-nun-ci-ate their words. One great benefit of practice is consciously working on both pace and enunciation.

4. Speak loudly enough for all to hear. While it's not necessary to shout, it's important to project to all hearers. If you doubt your projection, ask, as you begin speaking, if those in the far reaches of the room can hear. Adjust your voice level as necessary. This procedure also goes if you are wearing a microphone or speaking into one.

5. Maintain eye contact with all segments of your audience. Inexperienced speakers often let their eyes drift to one side of the room or the other; some even focus on one or two listeners and ignore the rest. Making *each and every person* in a room feel that you are talking to her or him takes conscious practice. One reason that we so strongly advise against reading a talk is that it eliminates the vital element of eye contact—unless the speaker is very experienced at maintaining eye contact while reading.

6. Move as you speak. Every speaking situation allows a different amount and kind of appropriate movement. A TV talk-show host routinely moves around a studio and from row to row among the audience; a graduation speaker stands behind a solid wood podium and speaks into a mike; an attorney questioning a witness is free to move around the courtroom, but the witness must stay put; and so on. In no case, however, must any speaker try to imitate a statue. Nevertheless, most inexperienced speakers miss chances to keep their audiences engaged through relevant movement.

Shifting eye contact and making moderate use of hand gestures are the most common moves that speakers use to keep their hearers' eyes attentive. But don't ignore the benefits of some moderate walking around a "speaking space" to keep your listeners engaged. Good teacher-lecturers routinely move from one side of a room to another, often writing down key ideas or pointing to terms already on a board or overhead. Business presenters do the same.

Even if you find yourself in a very rigidly defined space, or even if every preceding speaker has stood like a statue, don't hesitate to wake up your audience by doing something at least slightly different. Another benefit of having graphics tools such as a flip chart or overhead projector is that they give you a valid excuse for moving, even when others have been rooted to the spot.

7. Remember to breathe. This may seem a nonsensical suggestion, but the tense speaker often fails to breathe normally, with a consequent loss of composure, stamina, and volume. Speech trainers often use the formula "one thought, one breath": they urge their clients to take a breath at the end of each clause and sentence. Good breathing helps pacing, too.

8. Warm up before going on. Just as singers loosen their vocal chords by doing exercises before performing, speakers should warm up their voices by practicing a small portion of the talk just before the official speech. This warm-up can save you the embarrassment of a scratchy or cracked voice or of stumbling over syllables at the start of the talk.

9. Involve your audience. We've suggested many ways of keeping your audience attentive to your talk, but the best way is to encourage some type of response or input from them, at least occasionally. The best-known example of the interactive method of speaking is the **Socratic method,** so called because Plato's dialogues of the teaching of Socrates in fifth-century B.C.E. Athens illustrated this method. The Socratic speaker relies on frequent questions to the audience (as in the **Q-and-A method** described earlier). But what distinguishes the Socratic method is that the speaker really does expect an answer from the audience—though not one that will cause the speaker to drift from the topic. For example, the speaker presenting the talk on media representations of mental illness might throw out a statistical question to the audience: "Now what might you guess would be the average number of residents in a neighborhood group home in the United States?" Such a question piques the audience's interest because the speaker is putting them on the spot. To make the technique work, the speaker must be sure to leave enough time for one or more people in the audience to respond before moving on with the talk. Another typical "involving" move is to ask audiences for a quick show of hands—"How many of you have seen the movie _____?" In short, do anything you can do to keep your listeners actively involved in your topic and paying respectful, close heed to *you.*

10. Observe other speakers. In whatever situation you may be, look closely for techniques that make good talkers good. Whenever you find that a speaker is holding your attention, chances are that it's as much the result of engaging technique as of interesting content.

FURTHER SOURCES WE SUGGEST

Beebe, S., & Beebe, S. (1997). *Public speaking: An audience-centered approach.* Boston: Allyn & Bacon.

Gamble, T., & Gamble, M. (1994). *Public speaking in the age of diversity.* Boston: Allyn & Bacon.

Grice, G., & Skinner, J. (1995). *Mastering public speaking.* Boston: Allyn & Bacon.

Robbins, J. (1997). *High-impact presentations: A multimedia approach.* New York: J. Wiley.

Smith, T. (1991). *Making successful presentations: A self-teaching guide.* New York: J. Wiley.

Sullivan, R., & Wircenski, J. (1996). *Technical presentation workbook: Winning strategies for effective public speaking.* New York: ASME Press.

Zeuschner, R. (1997). *Communicating today.* Boston: Allyn & Bacon.

8

BRIEF APA CITATION GUIDE

The following guide to citation using the format prescribed by the American Psychological Association (APA) is meant to describe most types of citations used in both the text and reference sections of a manuscript. While the guide is not meant to be exhaustive, readers will find that almost all types of references they will ever use are described in these pages. For less common types of references, please see the *Publication Manual of the American Psychological Association*, fourth edition.

CITING SOURCES WITHIN THE TEXT OF A MANUSCRIPT (NO DIRECT QUOTATIONS)

A Source with a Single Author

You should cite the author's last name and the date of publication. If the author's name is part of the text, the date is given in parentheses: Smith (1999) concluded that. . . . If the author's name is presented in parentheses, you should insert a comma after the name: (Smith, 1999). You may also present the name and date as part of the narrative: In 1999, Smith concluded that. . . . The same citation should be used throughout the text. The only exception occurs when the same reference appears more than once in a paragraph. In this case, only the name (not the date) is given in all references after the first. This exception is true for all types of references; the date is always omitted after the first citation in a paragraph regardless of the number of authors of the article, book, or book title cited. Page numbers are not included unless the citation includes a direct quotation (see later).

A Source with Two Authors

You should cite both authors' last names and the date of publication throughout the text. If the reference is part of the text, the names are separated by *and:* Smith and Jones (1999) concluded that. . . . If the names are parenthetical, an ampersand (&) is used in place of the word *and:* (Smith & Jones, 1999).

A Source with Three to Five Authors

You should cite all authors' last names and the date of publication for the first citation of the reference. (The format is the same as described for two authors.) Commas are used between all names: Smith, Jones, and Johnson (1999) . . . if the reference appears as part of the text; (Smith, Jones, & Johnson, 1999) if the reference is parenthetical. On the second and subsequent citations in the text, only the first author's last name is given, followed by *et al.:* Smith et al. (1999) . . . if the reference appears as part of the text; (Smith et al., 1999) if the reference is parenthetical.

A Source with at Least Six Authors

You should cite only the last name of the first author, followed by *et al.* and the date for all citations, including the first. The reference appears in the text in the same format on second and subsequent citations. (*Note:* The entire reference, including all names, appears in the reference section of the manuscript.)

Two Sources by the Same Author(s) in the Same Year

If a paper references two or more sources by the same author or authors in the same year, lower-case letters *a, b, c,* etc. are added after the date to indicate the appropriate reference. The letter *a* should be assigned to the reference for which the first word of the title appears first alphabetically, *b* to the reference for which the title's first word appears second alphabetically: Smith (1999a) and (Smith 1999b) . . . or (Smith, 1999a, 1999b).

Group or Corporate Authorship

If an organization, rather than an individual, is cited, the full name is provided in the first citation and an abbreviation is presented in brackets. For all subsequent citations, only the abbreviation is used. For example, the first citation of a reference to the National Organization of Women would be (National Organization of Women [NOW], 1999); the second would be (NOW, 1999).

An Anonymous Reference

In citing a reference for which only a title is available, provide the title and underline it as the reference in the text. For example, a reference to "Undergraduate Student Handbook" would be presented as (Undergraduate Student Handbook).

Personal Communications

If the source of the information being cited is a personal communication (i.e., from an unpublished source), the term *personal communication* is included in parentheses. Because personal communications cannot be accessed by readers, no citation is included in the reference section of the text. The precise date should be included, if available: (H. R. Smith, personal communication, May 3, 1999.) Personal communications include face-to-face discussion as well as letters and telephone and electronic mail messages.

Two or More Sources Cited Together

If two or more sources are cited together, they should be written consecutively within the same parentheses. Semicolons are included to separate references. The format for individual citations is the same as described earlier, and the order of appearance is alphabetical by authors' last names. If one reference has a single author and another has multiple authors with the same last name as a single-author reference, the single-author reference appears first: (Jones, 1999; Smith, 1999; Smith & Jones, 1999). If a textual citation includes two or more references to the same author(s) in different years, the earlier one is placed first: (Smith, 1999, 2000).

Two Authors with the Same Last Name

If two or more authors with the same last name are both cited, the first initial of each author (or, if necessary to discriminate among them, the first and middle initials) is included in every citation: (A. Smith, 1999; H. A. Smith, 1999; H. R. Smith, 1999).

CITING DIRECT QUOTATIONS

Page numbers for references identified in the text of a manuscript appear only when direct quotations are given. Otherwise, the pages in which an article, book chapter, or other excerpt appears are given only in the reference section. For format purposes, the APA manual differentiates short and long quotations.

Short Quotations (up to 40 words)

If a quotation includes fewer than 40 words, it is included as part of the text. Quotation marks are included, and a page number is given. The author's (or authors') name(s) and date may either be given in the text before the quotation with the page number following the quotation, or the name(s), date, and page number may be given in parentheses after the quotation appears. An example of the first format is:

Smith (1999) defined knowledge as "how we, as human
beings, think, know, understand, discriminate, and
generalize" (p. 43).

An example of the second format is:

She defined knowledge as "how we, as human beings,
think, know, understand, discriminate, and generalize"
(Smith, 1999, p. 43).

Long Quotations (40 or more words)

If a quotation includes at least 40 words, it is separated from the rest of text by indenting five spaces from the left and blocking. (The right margin is not changed.) No quotation marks are included. The author's name is placed before the quotation, and the page number appears at the end. Here is an example:

Smith (1999) described knowledge in the following way:
    Knowledge can be defined as how we, as human beings,
    think, know, understand, discriminate, and

generalize. But each of these is a very complex
topic, and all are interrelated. For example,
discrimination and generalization are often thought
of as polar opposites, but one clearly affects the
other. Discrimination limits generalization by our
understanding that different inputs produce
different outcomes. (p. 43)

CITING SOURCES IN A REFERENCE SECTION

Alphabetizing and Spacing

In all references cited in the Reference section of a paper or other manuscript published using APA format, the reference list is alphabetized by the
last names of first authors. If two authors have the same last name, alpha-
betizing is completed by the initial of the first name (or initials of the first
and middle names, if necessary). In all cases, only the last names together
with the initials of the author's (or authors') first and middle names are
given; first and middle names are never written out. If the same author is
cited in two or more references, the order of presentation in the reference
section is determined by date of publication, with earlier publications preceding later ones. If the same author is cited in two or more references published in the same year, small letters *a, b, c,* etc., are added, with *a* the
reference in which the first word of the title appears first alphabetically.
**The references in the text and those cited in the reference section must
always match exactly.** Please also keep in mind that like all parts of a
manuscript published in APA style and format, the reference section is
double spaced. No extra spacing is included between successive references.

Capitalizing

The first letter of all authors' last names and the initials of the first and
middle names are capitalized in citations in the reference section of a manuscript. Also capitalized are the first words appearing after each of the two
periods in a reference, the first letter of a word appearing after a colon in
the title of the manuscript, the first letter of the first word of a book title, the
important words in the name of a journal (but not the title of the article
cited from the journal), the first words in the city and country of publication

(for states, the two-letter U.S. Postal Service abbreviation is used: "NY"), and the first letter of each important word in the name of the publisher. Unlike many other formats, APA does *not* capitalize all important words in the title of a journal article or book.

\Ordering Items within a Reference

Most citations consist of either journal articles, books, or book chapters, and all references in the reference section of a paper, regardless of their source, have common characteristics. In all cases, the author's (or authors') name(s) always appears first, and the first line is indented. The date of publication, placed in parentheses and followed by a period, appears after the name of the final author. Then the title of the article, book, or book chapter appears, followed by a period. A book title is underlined, but the title of a journal article or book chapter is typed without underlining.

In a reference to a journal article, the article title is followed by the name of the journal, a comma, the volume number of the journal, and another comma (all underlined). Finally, the page numbers on which the article appears (not underlined) are presented, and a period ends the reference.

If the reference is to a book, the city of publication, followed by a colon and the name of the publisher and a period, completes the reference. If the city is not well known as a center for publication, the abbreviation of the state (if the city is in the U.S.) or country (if the city is not in the U.S.) is also included. If the reference is to a book chapter, the chapter title is followed by the name(s) of the book's author(s) or editor(s), followed by a comma. The abbreviation "Ed(s)." appears in parentheses after the editor's (or editors') names(s) when citing edited works. Following this, the title of the book (underlined) and the pages on which the chapter appears (in parentheses and not underlined) are presented, followed by a period. Finally, like the book reference just described, the city (and sometimes the state or country) of publication appears.

The following sample reference list illustrates the points made above. Reference sections in the sample laboratory report (Chapter 3) and term paper (Chapter 4) also portray the format that has been described.

Sample Reference List

Here are examples of different types of references that appear in the reference section of a published work. These references are not to published material; they are for illustrative purposes only.

Journal Article, Single Author

Johnson, Q. L. (2000). Toward a definition of thought: A biological perspective. <u>The Chicago Journal of Applied Psychology, 55,</u> 412-430.

Please note in this example the order in which different parts of the reference appear, the words that are capitalized, and the underlining. As described in the preceding paragraphs, the order consists of author, date of publication, article title, journal, volume number, *and* page numbers. *The author's name, the first letter of the article title, the first letter after a colon in the title, and the first letter of each important word in the name of the journal are capitalized. However, other words in the title are not capitalized. The name of the journal and the volume number (through the comma following it) are continuously underlined.*

Journal Article, Multiple Authors

Johnson, Q. L., Carmody, B. V., & Dunn, D. D. (2000). The schizophrenic mind. <u>The Chicago Journal of Applied Psychology, 55,</u> 448-460.

Note that commas appear after each author's name, including the name preceding the ampersand (&).

Magazine or Newsletter Article

Dunn, D. D. (1999, October). Schizophrenia in public schools. <u>The Vermont Elementary Educator, 12,</u> 99-103.

Note that the date of publication includes the date as it appears on the issue. This example shows a monthly publication and an October date. Had this been a seasonal or weekly publication, the season (e.g., Autumn*) or the precise date (e.g.,* October 16*) would have appeared.*

Book Chapter

Johnson, Q. L., & Williams, Z. (1999). Discrimination and generalization: Two sides of the same coin. In X. T. Smith (Ed.), <u>Biological and</u>

<u>psychological bases of thought</u> (pp. 42-52). London: PsycPress.

As described earlier, only the first letter of the first word of book and book chapter titles is capitalized. The title of the book is underlined, and the pages on which the chapter can be found are included in the reference.

Two References by the Same Authors in the Same Year

Johnson, Q. L., & Fox, L. L. (1999a). Concepts and their mediation. <u>Journal of Language and Linguistic Processes, 32,</u> 157-169.

Johnson, Q. L., & Fox, L. L. (1999b). Thought and generalization. <u>Journal of Language and Linguistic Processes, 32,</u> 136-156.

Note that since concepts *precedes* thought *alphabetically,* a *is assigned to the reference that begins with the word* concepts.

Book

Smith, A. B. C. (1999). <u>An introduction to thought processes.</u> Fairfax, VA: PQR Press.

Group or Corporate Authorship

National Congress for Women. (2000). <u>An update on the status of women in the new millennium</u> [Brochure]. Washington, DC: New Press.

Note that the type of publication (in this case, a brochure) is identified.

Later Editions of Books

Layman, P. R. (1999). <u>The state of psychology</u> (4th ed.). London: PsycPress.

The number of the edition (after the first) is always given for any book.

Translated Book

> Pierpont, B. X. (2000). <u>Animal languages</u> (G. B. Hovering, Trans.). Philadelphia: Ethology Press. (Original work published 1925)

Note that the translator is identified in parentheses. In the text, both the original publication date and the date of translation are included: "Pierpont (1925/2000)."

Technical/Research Reports

> Parker, S. S., Quinlan, A. L., & Short, S. T. (2000). <u>Effects of alcohol on multiple choice test performance</u> (VSCSA Rep. No. 00-55). Richmond, VA: Virginia State Council on Substance Abuse.

The information in parentheses after the report title identifies the source and number of the report. Almost all organizations that produce technical and research reports include an abbreviation that represents the name of the organization and a number that identifies the particular report. Sometimes, as in this example, the number identifies the year of publication (00 represents the year 2000).

Proceedings of a Conference

> Layman, P. R. (2000). Where are we going: Psychology's next paradigm shift. <u>Proceedings of the Great Lakes Association on the Future of Psychology,</u> <u>15,</u> 433-443.

The word Proceedings *identifies this reference as conference proceedings. As you can see, the format is very similar to that of a journal article.*

Poster Session

> Masters, L. A., & Parker, S. S. (2000, March). <u>Alcohol and standardized tests: Effects of minimal dosage on speed of response.</u> Poster session presented at the annual meeting of the Virginia State Council Conference on Alcohol, Richmond, VA.

The month as well as the year is commonly included in references to posters presented at conferences.

Unpublished Doctoral Dissertations

Schooling, I. W. (1999). <u>Effects of aging on memory of early childhood events.</u> Unpublished doctoral dissertation, George Mason University, Fairfax, VA.

Book/Film/etc. Review

Bradling, G. H. (2001). Whither Y2K? [Review of the book <u>Looking back at the psychological effects of Y2K</u>]. <u>BPR Review of Books and Films, 14,</u> 345–348.

Note that the type of medium (book, film, etc.) is identified in brackets.

Online Abstract

Robbins, L. A, & Breech, Y. P. (2000). Birth order and the development of a second language. [Online]. <u>South African Journal of Second Language Acquisition, 67,</u> 345–365. Abstract from NIMAX: PSYCHPro #999-66741

The bracketed information identifies the reference as coming from an online source. Note that the reference does not end with a period (to assist in source retrieval).

Encyclopedia/Dictionary

Froth, L. Y. et al. (Ed.). (1999). <u>The California music therapy encyclopedia</u> (3rd ed.). Fullerton, CA: MTP.

Nearly all encyclopedias and dictionaries will have an editor or editors. If a large number are listed, the citation includes the name of only the first, followed by et al.

REFERENCES

Alba, J. W., & Hasher, L. (1983). Is memory schematic? *Psychological Bulletin, 93,* 203–231.

American Psychological Association. (1994). *Publication manual of the American Psychological Association* (4th ed.). Washington, DC: Author.

Craik, F. I. M., & Lockhart, R. S. (1972). Levels of processing: A framework for memory research. *Journal of Verbal Learning and Verbal Behavior, 11,* 671–684.

Haberlandt, K. (1997). *Cognitive psychology* (2nd ed.). Needham Heights, MA: Allyn & Bacon.

Hult, C. A., & Huckin, T. N. (1999). *The new century handbook.* Needham Heights, MA: Allyn & Bacon.

Martin, D. W. (1996). *Doing psychology experiments* (4th ed.). Pacific Grove, CA: Brooks/Cole.

Murray, D. M. (1995). *The craft of revision.* Fort Worth, TX: Harcourt Brace.

Rogers, T. B., Kuiper, N. A., & Kirker, W. S. (1977). Self-reference and the encoding of personal information. *Journal of Personality and Social Psychology, 35,* 677–688.

INDEX

ABOUT THE AUTHORS

Christopher Thaiss is Professor of English at George Mason University, where he chairs the department and has served as Director of English Composition and Writing across the Curriculum. A consultant on the teaching of writing across the disciplines for almost twenty years, he has authored or edited eight books, including *The Harcourt Brace Guide to Writing across the Curriculum* (1998), and, for Allyn & Bacon, *Writing about Theatre* (with Rick Davis) and *Writing for Law Enforcement* (with John E. Hess), both published in 1999.

James F. Sanford is Associate Chair for Undergraduate Studies in the Department of Psychology at George Mason University. He has recently developed an email mentoring program linking advanced psychology majors with freshmen enrolled in introductory psychology and a unique service learning program for psychology undergraduates. His research interests include memory and cognition and mentoring processes in higher education. He has long been active in the university's Writing across the Curriculum Program.